MATERNAL AMBIVALENCE

Also by Margo Lowy, PhD

*The Maternal Experience: Encounters
with Ambivalence and Love*

MATERNAL AMBIVALENCE

The Loving Moments and
Bitter Truths of Motherhood

MARGO LOWY, PHD

A POST HILL PRESS BOOK
ISBN: 979-8-88845-598-2
ISBN (eBook): 979-8-88845-599-9

Post Hill Press
New York • Nashville
posthillpress.com

Published in the United States of America
1 2 3 4 5 6 7 8 9 10

*For my children, Daniel, Noah, and Milz,
who I love deeply and from whom I've
learned the power of surrendering.*

*To suffer with and for and against a child—
maternally, egotistically, neurotically, sometimes
with a sense of helplessness, sometimes in
the illusion of learning wisdom—but always,
everywhere, in body and soul, with that child—
because that child is a piece of oneself.*

—ADRIENNE RICH, *Of Woman Born*

*All mothering, whether in family or
individual, is made up of both affectionate
caring and bitter emotional pain.*

—THOMAS MOORE, *Care of the Soul*

CONTENTS

ambivalence
US /æmˈbɪv.ə.ləns/ UK /æmˈbɪv.ə.ləns/

noun [U]
the state of having two opposing feelings at the same time, or being uncertain about how you feel.
—*Cambridge English Dictionary*

ambivalence
am·biv·a·lence | \ am-ˈbi-və-lən(t)s

noun
1: simultaneous and contradictory attitudes or feelings (such as attraction and repulsion) toward an object, person, or action
2a: continual fluctuation (as between one thing and its opposite)
b: uncertainty as to which approach to follow
—*Merriam-Webster Dictionary*

ambivalence
/æmˈbɪvələns/

noun
the fact of having or showing both positive and negative feelings about somebody/something
—*Oxford English Dictionary*

Maternal ambivalence
an "experience shared variously by all mothers in which loving and hating feelings for their children exist side by side."
—Rozsika Parker, *Torn in Two*

INTRODUCTION

DO WE REALLY NEED ANOTHER book about mothering? Not especially—there are plenty. Actually, the market is saturated with them, not to mention the overwhelming noisiness of advice and criticism available online and on social media. It seems that the last thing anyone needs is another Christmas stocking stuffer or baby shower gift. So why have I written this one?

Because there is an aspect of mothering that isn't yet really understood and needs to be. It's crucial to our mothering and to most of the interactions that we have with our children. It occurs nearly every day, to nearly every mother on this planet, and it isn't addressed in books on parenting and raising happy, healthy, well-adjusted children. It doesn't get airspace on mommy blogs and Facebook forums. Not many people talk about it because they aren't sure what it means, and they are confused by its taboo language, so they avoid it. In it lies the truth that we have conflicting feelings about our mothering and that we don't know how to talk about it. Our days with our children are often difficult, repetitive, boring, mindless, and leave us at our wits' end. We often feel squeezed out, scared by our own sense of hopelessness—sometimes there's just no ray of light. Motherhood is relentless, and it forces many of us to lie about our true feelings, to admit we're not perfect. If we confess that we don't love our children every minute of every day, or that sometimes we are only pretending to, then we also have to believe that there is something not right about us as mothers. Of course, the truth is far from this.

This scarcely named dynamic is known as maternal ambivalence. It's the essence of mothering—a mother's acceptance of her contradictory feelings about her child. It relies on her capacity to choose flow over rigidity. It lies in her understanding that her days hold a multitude of feelings, including joy, resentment, tenderness, exhaustion, anger, irritation, humor, tears, pain, panic, fear, suffering, soothing, elation, and sometimes even pangs of hatred. Despite this reality, we don't yet have a language that brings these conflicting feelings together and gives the troubling feelings a rightful place. We need words, and a language, that normalize all the mother's emotions and encourage her to somehow hold them together. While we tend to prioritize the mother's loving feelings, we are unsure about what to do with the troubling ones, so we go to a default position. This means we usually push the disturbing ones down because they are just too much and they remind us that both our child and ourselves are flawed. What we don't realize is that the tension between these conflicting emotions actually keeps us going. It renews and transforms us. And even the most distressing, messy, ugly, and unspeakable feelings have value. In owning them and trying to understand rather than dismissing them, our mothering becomes more truthful and real. All our feelings have worth when we learn from them. This is the power that is maternal ambivalence, and it's the heart of this book.

This idea did not surface spontaneously for me one day. I've long understood, from my own experience and those of mothers around me, that a substantial untapped area of mothering exists. As a psychotherapist, I have continually witnessed a symbolic empty seat reserved for the mother in many sessions with my clients. Whether Mom or Mum, she always had a presence somewhere in the room. While I could find a lot written about mothering from a psychological and social perspective, I knew that something was missing: a connection, a key understanding more about the real, yet unspoken, lived experience of being a mother. So I started a search for something new about mothering that would explain this gap. While trawling the literature, I found Rozsika Parker's book *Torn in Two*,[1] and the notion of maternal ambivalence entered my life.

Parker, the groundbreaking writer on the subject of maternal ambivalence, defines it as "the experience shared variously by all mothers in which loving and hating feelings for their children exist side by side,"[2] radically naming hatred as part of a mother's everyday experience and regarding it as a creative energy. She went further by describing "the fleeting (or not so fleeting) feelings of hatred for a child that can grip a mother, the moment of recoil from a much-loved body, the desire to abandon, to smash the untouched plate of food in a toddler's face, to yank a child's arm while crossing the road, scrub too hard with a facecloth, change the lock against an adolescent, or the fantasy of hurling a howling baby out of the window."[3] My research into Parker's and others' work allowed me to re-envision the daily experience of motherhood for myself as both a mother and a therapist. It led me to discover a version of mothering that is more truthful and organic and less a reflection of social "norms." Maternal ambivalence encourages us as mothers to own all our feelings and to claim our own genuine voice, the one that belongs to us, rather than the one society expects us to have. My approach will, hopefully, help to change how society dictates the ways a mother is supposed to act and allow her to more honestly acknowledge the feelings she has toward herself and her child, resulting in a more forgiving and nourishing relationship with her child.

Parker's work both shocked and intrigued me. I could get my head around the transformative element of the mother's distressing feelings, but the word "hate" is so disturbing. It's totally out of our comfort zone—outside of only the most extreme circumstances, hatred is a taboo. However, once I let go of my own moralizing and judgment and began to think as critically and objectively as I could about what Parker was really saying, I was able to reach some clarity. I have refined Parker's account of hatred as one that is nestled exclusively in the context of maternal love. It is not a static state, rather it is a passing moment. It is fluid. It is a feeling not an action. I've witnessed many different responses to the suggestion of maternal hate: paralysis, shock, anger, and also nods of recognition and relief. While as a society we may not yet be comfortable with this seemingly counterintuitive dynamic, albeit within the complexity of maternal love, we need to free ourselves of the ways we've been conditioned to think about mothering—to give ourselves an opportunity to rethink mothering and how we define a "good" mother.

After more than ten years of formulating my ideas about maternal ambivalence—earning a doctorate and writing an academic book along the way—I've found a huge gap in the literature and the advice culture of mothering where an understanding of it needs to live. There aren't enough experts reassuring mothers that these feelings of maternal ambivalence exist, much less that they are normal—and navigable. In fact, they are valuable and essential to an understanding of a mother's everyday life. Rather than hiding or denying these feelings, or living in shame and guilt for having them, the conversation about maternal ambivalence needs to be discussed widely—without stigma or fear of committing social suicide. Maternal ambivalence encourages the mother to embrace all of her moods and emotions fully. This does not mean acting on them; it means understanding, acknowledging, and processing them. This book is aimed at disrupting long-held beliefs about what a mother *should* be. Everyone seems to have a stake in, and a comment about, what mothers should or shouldn't be. There's that word again. I have an uneasy relationship with this word and the notion of "should," as I consider that it moralizes. I try to minimize its use in the book, but when it appears, it is in the least judgmental way.

What is maternal ambivalence? It might be easier to return to the source, to begin with a definition of ambivalence itself. Ambivalence is the coexistence in one person of opposite and conflicting feelings toward someone or something. When we honestly reflect on our feelings and exchanges with others, there are usually multiple emotions involved. We may admit, for example, that while we adore someone, they also annoy us. There are dark and light shades to everyone's character or behavior. The sting lies in the reality that the closer we are with someone, the more fraught and complicated our feelings and exchanges are, the more often we are triggered, the more sensitive we seem to be. So we can only imagine that in this context, feelings about mothering sometimes go off the charts. Ambivalence exists in all relationships, and its value comes from being able to stay with our contradictory feelings and not reject the difficult ones. It exists in most everyday experiences, and if we can get a general understanding of it, this can help us with our mothering and our daily life.

To illustrate maternal ambivalence, I will share a few stories:

Picture a new mom who is totally exhausted from getting up five times during the night with her infant. He has been screaming and pulling at his ears, has red cheeks, and will only settle when she holds him. She's thinking, "This little shit. I can't do this anymore. I need sleep." At 5 a.m., he takes some milk, gives a satisfied smile, and falls asleep on her. As she puts him gently into bed, she realizes he has a tooth coming in. She takes a moment to stare with wonder and utter love before she rolls into bed herself. This bittersweet feeling of exhaustion and love...this is maternal ambivalence. Let's not disregard the difficult parts of the total experience— these moments are what mothering is about, the melting moments, all part of renewing her love, knowing that she will be doing it all over again in a few hours.

Visualize the three-year-old toddler at the park with his mother and newborn sister. The mother reminds her son to stay close by and not to climb the slide while she changes her baby's diaper. After sixty seconds, she turns around to check on him, and she cannot find him. She looks up and sees him at the top of the slide, and is overcome with feelings of fear as she imagines him lying motionless on the ground after he falls. Somehow she manages to calmly climb up the steps of the slide as she coaxes him not to move, and she reaches the top and grabs his hand. At this moment, she is deluged with feelings including anger, relief, resentment, gratitude, and even flashes of hate, which strengthen the overpowering love that she feels at that moment.

Mom is called to school for the third time this month. Last week, her thirteen-year-old was sliding down the stairs on a suitcase at an excursion, and he broke a chair. The week before, he had been disruptive in class and wasn't doing his homework. She's wondering, "Where have I gone wrong?" and "What's he done now?" "What's his punishment this time? I have run out of ideas." "I'm over all this." When he doesn't come to meet her at the school office, she is furious. Then the nurse comes and tells her that he has a black eye after defending his mate, who was being bullied in a fight. She melts with love. She judged him—again. He's so amazing; he's just out of the mold. She hugs him, and they laugh together as he shows her his black eye.

Then there's the eighteen-year-old who is moving further away from her mother every day. She's out all day with her friends. Mom misses her and is worried because she isn't answering her phone. She comes in late at night and gives her mother a big hug and kiss before saying, "Sorry, Mom, I was in that school meeting so my phone was off. Remember, I told you this morning. I love you. You are the best." That's enough. These little moments recharge our love.

The next stage of mothering is a new experience. We get to watch our children become adults, and new challenges arise. We have to get comfortable with them moving away from us and forging their new ways of being. We must learn to hold our tongues, to witness and not to comment, to observe as they make and repair their mistakes. We experience ambivalence as we take a step back; we watch and continue to care, but we don't advise unless asked. We both enjoy and are in pain for and with our children, but it's their turn now. This is a huge adjustment as we learn to live with those benefits while they mature and their struggles and strains evolve.

This is maternal ambivalence: the moments that both confront and melt us, and the troubling, discomfiting feelings—those such as disappointment, anger, pity, fatigue—which all meld into and strengthen our love. The exchanges above illustrate so much of the everyday experience of being a mother, the fleeting feelings that affect her so deeply. Maternal ambivalence upsets so many of our expectations for motherhood, particularly that we will love our children wholly and unconditionally from the moment they are born. In fact, the first trauma a mother often experiences is feelings of frustration toward her newborn. When her baby can't stop crying, she feels out of control. She can't fix the situation, and she's exhausted. Sleeplessness puts her on the edge of sanity. She is briefly filled with resentment and helplessness, though she knows her baby isn't doing this on purpose. After she processes the occurrence—she returns to her mothering and the realization that incidents like this will happen time and again and she must steel herself for them and hope that her love will continue to be renewed and strengthened. When she admits to her distressing feelings, she locates some reality and peace for herself.

These are the sort of disturbing-yet-commonplace events that happen every day while raising children. They remind us how much we love our child *and* how much damn work it takes to be a parent. It takes some of us a lifetime to understand the complexities of motherhood.

Every mother experiences these contradictory feelings about mothering over her years of parenting. Some can admit to this freely. Some are outraged at the suggestion that they might feel any ill will toward their children. And still others reflect that they've just never thought about the challenges of parenting that way. A lot of mothers hide from these feelings, attempt to ignore or quash them, and hope that they'll disappear, even as they are aware that they won't. The experience of these feelings can have an unbalancing and troubling effect on any mother. A mother who denies them altogether often finds herself trapped in a web of guilt, shame, and rigidity. Despite these barriers, I know that the love we have for our children is vast enough to harbor many uncomfortable, and at times even odious, emotions for the ever-changing experience that is mothering. Human emotions are fluid, and language is likewise flowing and also forgiving.

The writing of this book is a culmination of many years of examining this misunderstood, taboo, and sidelined maternal dynamic. Paradoxically, this silenced part of mothering is central and an everyday experience. I encourage every mother to claim all her feelings and find a way to become comfortable with them, in a style that fits her, that is her own. By naming and leaning into her true feelings, hopefully she can learn to better navigate any kind of judgment linked with them that surfaces from inside her or from the outside world and, as a result, become the best mother that she can be.

This book is the start of a new language of mothering. I encourage everyone, mothers and children of mothers, which we all are, to invent, own, and name a language of their own with ambivalence as a core element. Mothering is a mosaic of feelings and experiences. It's not only a full-time job; it's a 24/7 emotional and physical enterprise. There are times when it's happy and successful—and then there are other moments. When all of its facets are honestly examined and lived, any mother must be prepared to recognize and take responsibility for all her feelings. While having children is the most creative and life-affirming act for many women, a connected mother is also open to the continual experience of suffering and pain as well as joy. Her uncomfortable, conflicting feelings are underexamined. While engaging with contradictory and upsetting emotions, by trying to understand and talk about them, an opportunity for transformation and a more fulfilling relationship between herself and her child is possible. By naming these contradictions, we can free the mother to examine and confront her taboo feelings. My greatest hope is that this book joins the relatively small number that have questioned the traditional taboos and stigmas surrounding motherhood and shines a light on their absolute normalcy. Parker's work, and that of the handful of others who have come before me, has opened my eyes to the value of recognizing all the mother's feelings, especially the painful and difficult ones, together with the contrary idea that these uncomfortable emotions actually fuel her love. I have spent many years advocating for the place of maternal ambivalence in the maternal language.

Every person has a story; every mother has her own experience. In this book, mothers will no doubt find their own moments of love, shame, guilt, humor, anger, and frustrations to identify with. While many forces within the mother, and in wider society, conspire to stymie the development of a robust discourse about maternal feelings of ambivalence, one of the intentions of this book is to expose the normalcy of these feelings and to contribute to the continuity of the conversation. My other intention is to help any mother—or parent, grandparent, or child-carer—to achieve an understanding of maternal ambivalence. It is a messy, sometimes frightening and painful, uphill climb, but at its pinnacle is the reward of resilience, love, even happiness and laughter—the best version of oneself possible. I will be here to guide you, validate your feelings, help you to redefine the complex expectations of motherhood, and to find the words and language to understand all of the joys and challenges that mothering holds. The dialogue begins here.

ONE

WHAT IS MATERNAL AMBIVALENCE?

EVERYONE HAS A MOTHER. As I wrote in my first book, every person, living or dead, was born to a mother. A child's emotional awareness of a mother's presence and absence endures in his or her mind, as he or she negotiates the emotions that this connection, or lack thereof, provokes. One's inner psyche is deeply affected by one's relationship with one's mother. The mother-and-child relationship is our most primal human connection, a child's first playground. Author Hester Solomon, in David Mann's anthology *Love and Hate*,[4] describes a mother and her infant as the "first couple in love—the first loving couple: the mother and her infant, and the infant and its mother—which form the basis of all later exchanges."[5] It is a cyclical relationship in which mother and child continually influence one another. An infant cries, and a mother responds with feeding or holding; a mother soothes, and her child recognizes her voice and stops crying. A child cannot exist without its mother; a mother is bound by love to care for her offspring.

Let's talk about what we aren't really allowed to say, though. It's not a simple relationship; rather, it's one of the most complex and least understood. Motherhood is the most extreme form of life's expressions, creating and giving birth to a brand-new human being. For many, having a child is their life's meaning. It's also the greatest of life's challenges. If we're being real here, motherhood sometimes sucks. Along with the anticipated feelings of deep love, enjoyment, warmth, humor, delight, and connection, there is exasperation, irritation, rage, loss, anguish, shame, despair, and remorse. It is a psychic puzzle. Sometimes these feelings occur over a lifetime; many mothers will tell you that they're all guaranteed to occur during an hour at the park, in the middle of a busy supermarket, and almost always at bedtime. Mothers are often at a loss with how to deal with their troublesome, painful feelings, which can be overwhelming and even shocking, and which are of course combined with sleepless nights and the ever-present stress of keeping a child well fed, warm, and healthy. This all creates a cycle of worry, shame, and desperation that seems impossible to escape. The more she worries, the more frantic she becomes, and nothing seems to work. She repeats her mistakes over many years of mothering, becoming stuck in the same behaviors, unable to learn from them and transform her perspective. We've all been there.

In our own lives, there is the ever-present background noise of expectations for the mother. Judgment flies in formation over our heads constantly, whether from the outside world or within. Historically, mothers have been painted in terms of either/or. She is either wonderful or terrible, caring or neglectful, loving or vicious. She is rarely seen as both, or as more than two-dimensional. She can be only angel or devil. This labeling system simply does not allow any mother the room she needs to make mistakes, to be flawed, or to explore her negative feelings in a meaningful way, to forgive herself or to feel forgiven. Everyone seems to have a stake in, and a comment about, what mothers should or shouldn't be. There's that word again, moralizing over the undisputed human condition.

Being a mom is so difficult some days. We are pulled in so many different directions by our children, and we are supposed to be caring, selfless, and remain an adult all the time, even when it becomes too much. How do we make room to acknowledge and talk about maternal ambivalence, a forbidden and silenced but daily part of our mothering?

Making sense of these contradictions in order to live with them in a peaceful and productive way may be the greatest challenge of all. As a mother of three, I've struggled—and still do—with my mothering. While my children are all things to me—the wonder, love, and accomplishment of my life—they also test me continually as I tread the awe, joy, and heartbreak of being a mother and its continual twists and turns. On that score, I'm not so different from any other mother.

I suppose my difference creeps in in the way that I have dealt with my experience of mothering and its combination of awe, joy, and heartbreak. It hasn't been easy, and why would it be? I have been driven to spend years of my life trying to find ways to make sense of mothering and the mother's feelings of ambivalence. I have pondered its contradictions and mystery while questioning the status quo and the wider social commentary. It seems to me that most people, both men and women, feel entitled to freely comment on the sacred feelings that a woman experiences as a mother, often leaving her with deep, unsettling feelings that may be hidden in the shadows or feel shameful. Ironically, this research and work on mothering began with a foray into infertility and the heartache that a woman usually feels when she is unable to conceive. My belief that these feelings are too important to ignore, too fragile to be denied, also segued into a desire to shine a light on the desperation that many mothers feel. Both infertility and mothering, in their own way, provoke a sense of failure or lacking, a yearning, and many negative feelings that go unspoken. Both hold an element of taboo. That's the fascination for me: the jumbling, contradictory flow of life.

This raises another matter, which is that this is not a book about whether or not to have children, despite the fact that maternal ambivalence is sometimes understood in these terms. To this point, I strongly believe that most women who decide not to have a child do not come to their decision lightly; more often than not, it arrives after a great deal of soul-searching. These women merit exactly the same respect as those who decide that they wish to rear a child; they don't justify derision or voicelessness. Across all cultures in this world, there is a universal truth, which is that motherhood defines womanhood in some way, whether we have children or not. We are judged for the ways in which we raise our children and judged when we choose not to raise them. Men and fathers, too, experience the conflict of parenthood and that dialogue, and while much different than it was even a half century ago, it still has much progress to make. My focus in this book, however, is the intersection of woman-hood and motherhood—the relationship that springs into being after birth and exists long after a child has left the nest.

Every mother has her moments when troubling feelings, including those of desperation, anger, loneliness, exhaustion, and despair, surface despite attempts to keep them down where she thinks that they belong. I think these moments have been disregarded or cloaked in denial. It's time to air and name them, and in doing so, redefine the image of a mother as either a demon or an angel into one where she is an ordinary human being—one who, despite having these feelings, does still love her child deeply and, in fact, within these troubling feelings, discovers that her love is strengthened and fueled in the soundest way possible because these feelings are genuine and real.

Ambivalence is the human capacity to acknowledge, own, and engage with many contradictory feelings, without dismissing the difficult ones. An indication of a healthy mindset is an acceptance that this dynamic is part of life, that challenges will crop up from time to time, and that the individual is prepared to work with them and not to dismiss or repress any of them. While the idea of ambivalence certainly throws many curveballs, let's welcome it: it's the unsung hero(ine) of mothering.

Maternal ambivalence conjures different ideas for different people. For some, it's impossible to accept the seeming paradox that sitting and struggling with contradictory feelings can be an achievement. Facing ambivalence often means letting go of the fantasy of being a "perfect" mother. It requires delving into that vault that we all hold inside ourselves, the one full of many different, secret emotions. In this space we often store our past, especially with our own mothers, our current life conditions and challenges, and all our personal stuff and unresolved issues—the deep unconscious process driving all our thoughts and feelings as we try just to get through each day with our kids.

This brings me to the Greek myth of Demeter, the goddess of the harvest, and her daughter Persephone, who has been abducted to the underworld by Hades, the god of the underworld. In this ancient story, Demeter embarks on a tumultuous journey to find and reclaim her daughter, who has been taken to the underworld while playing in the fields with her friends. This scenario presents countless possibilities and layers of interpretation. I use the lens of maternal ambivalence, which insists that the mother experiences many different and often conflicting feelings in her daily experiences, including dark, uncomfortable ones as well as loving ones, as a guide for me to find meaning in and learn from this myth.

On learning that her young, innocent daughter has been abducted to the underworld, Demeter sets off on a frantic search for her. The mother begins to lose her mind with worry. She neglects her work, the fields of the Earth are soon empty, and there is turmoil. At the same time, trapped in the underworld, Persephone misses her mother terribly and refuses to eat. The situation on Earth soon becomes so dreadful that Hades is convinced to return Persephone to her mother. However, before she goes, Hades persuades the girl to eat four pomegranate seeds, sentencing her to return to the underworld for four months each year. Demeter accepts this sentence, though these months bring her suffering and torment.

Demeter's story is not unique. Her delight at the return of her daughter soon turns to dismay as she realizes that, while her daughter is returned, both of their worlds have been altered. There are new rules. The young girl she left safely playing in the fields is no longer so innocent, and Demeter must let go of her initial dreams and re-envision her actuality. She is faced with a daughter who has a secret side now and who abandons her mother every year to go back to the darkness of the underworld. I imagine that Demeter experiences and struggles with many shocking and dark feelings as she considers her new reality, possibly including flashes of maternal hate, feelings of regret, sorrow, shame, guilt, and loss, and then overwhelming, strengthened feelings of love for Persephone.

This myth teaches us a lot about mothering. We must face the truth that it is not carried out on our terms and that any thought otherwise must be re-examined. It teaches us to let go of any expectation that the path with our child will be smooth and clear. It teaches us, too, that we need to be flexible, and that there is heartache and pain, but not all the time. That there is also, predominantly, joy. That our children may miss us, but they must lead their own lives. It teaches us that there are places where we cannot go that belong to them. Our children, like us, have their dark sides, and we must accept them if they are to come back to us. We must be forgiving. We must receive them as they are. We must surrender.

What can we learn from the story of Demeter? I regard her as a powerful symbol of maternal wisdom. I imagine that Persephone's disappearance and return with its unexpected twist forces Demeter to struggle with certain conflicting truths. Her daughter now moves between light and darkness, which reminds Demeter of her own darkness and the reality that she is not invited to know her daughter's secrets in the underworld. The mother must acknowledge that the world is full of unknowns and that she cannot protect her daughter fully or control her destiny. Her daughter has a mind of her own, and Demeter must concede that Persephone is separate from her. Persephone's decision to eat the pomegranate seeds shows us that our children will do things that we don't want them to and that sometimes they make foolish decisions, but we must accept that and move forward if we are to maintain a relationship with them.

We are reminded that mothering is full of loss, and we are forced to think about the expectations and dreams that we have for our children and how they are just that: illusions, not necessarily in step with reality. Demeter endures two losses: the first is an actual loss as Persephone is abducted to the underworld, and the second is a symbolic loss, as Persephone returns to Earth as a different daughter. The lesson in the myth is how Persephone's return brings both joy and disquiet for Demeter, who must now find renewed love and forgiveness for her daughter despite the young woman's liaisons in the underworld. While it is confronting, Demeter is aware that any further and meaningful connection with her daughter relies on her own earned wisdom and acceptance, on her capacity to surrender. The myth represents a mother's daily and numerous experiences of loss and renewal and the responsibility she carries to regulate herself and remain adult. It also traces that inevitable arc toward a child's independence, as the mother remains on the sidelines awaiting her child's return in due time. I understand this myth as an embodiment of Demeter's wisdom as she realizes that a future with her daughter lies in adapting to this new dynamic. She learns to live with change and to integrate her feelings of deep love with her other deep feelings of resentment, pity, anger, or passing flashes of hatred. This, again, is maternal ambivalence.

Ambivalence, the practice of holding and navigating through many different emotions simultaneously, some of which are contradictory, is an active experience. It is the practice of being inclusive, using *and*: I can feel tenderness and pain, happiness and despair, love and hate, joy and anger. This capacity to sit with uncomfortable feelings rather than rejecting them is much more difficult than it sounds. It is hard work, and it is often confusing. It's much easier to push away those feelings that upset us and to avoid confronting difficulties even within ourselves. However, being able to manage this kind of conflict is the mark of a mindfully developed person who can process and grasp more than one side of a situation.

From what I understand, Demeter actively avoids the temptation to cut herself off from either her joy or her displeasure or to judge her daughter; rather, she contends with the minefield of her feelings. By engaging with both sides of the situation, she is able to think in terms of the light and the darkness, the upside and the downside, rather than being limited to good or bad, right or wrong.

In the world we live in, of course, the drama of mothering doesn't always reach such mythic heights, but still, it has its moments. Mothering teenagers and young adults can be just as soul-wrenching an experience as mothering babies, sometimes more so. Take, for example, a mother collecting her sixteen-year-old daughter from a party. She experiences total relief and love now that her daughter is safely back with her. She also experiences fleeting feelings of anger, sometimes along with momentary pangs of hatred, as she realizes her daughter has been drinking alcohol after promising she would not. Any mother would be terrified to know her child has exposed herself to danger and furious that she has broken her promise. Compounding this mindset, as mothers we are often horrified by our experience of maternal ambivalence, gripped by the emotions of love and familiar dark feelings, knowing our children are venturing out beyond our control.

Motherhood is a messy, loving process, filled with complicated and conflicting feelings that, though it's hard to admit to, can even include passing moments of hate. The struggle a mother faces as she recognizes troublesome feelings equally allows her to discover new ways to engage with her child. This investigation of the mother within her social and psychic context brings an examination of her lived experience of maternal ambivalence in which all her emotions dwell together. When a mother can capture all her feelings, she is in the best place to access her losses and repair them. A mother's capacity for fluidity, as opposed to rigidity, is central to developing resilience as a parent and a person. The honest experience of all facets of maternal love is what inspires and instills maternal wisdom.

The old silent approach simply hasn't worked. And ignoring this fragile, vital part of mothering is neglecting a universal truth in every mother's daily life. There needs to be an open discussion of all maternal emotions so that a mother can find and access help when she is at her wits' end. Mothers need to talk about their full experience, and in the following chapters, many of them will.

We have a responsibility, to ourselves above all, to explore and own all our feelings and observe the tension that exists between opposing ones. By uncovering maternal ambivalence, we discover a safe place for fuller expression. Our ambivalence is an achievement well-earned rather than a failure to retreat from. I urge you to find your own words to own these complex and contradictory feelings. Naming them keeps us going as our conflicts and pain renew and fuel our love rather than depleting it. We evolve and transform. It's a win-win.

Motherhood is a paradox of loving and not-so-loving moments—hope and hopelessness, making mistakes and learning from them, independence through dependence, the unknown and familiar, pleasure and pain, laughter and tears, closeness and distance, expansion and contraction, gain and loss. I want to allow moms to accept and honor all of these experiences with honesty, self-love, and forgiveness, so we can all get on with our mothering in the way that we need to.

One of my main challenges has been to find a comfortable place to understand what we all know but are afraid to talk about—that dark, unspoken feelings exist as a daily part of our mothering; they belong to us. I wonder about these feelings, and I need to find words for them. To say them aloud and to hear them. To normalize and demystify them. As mothers, we must free ourselves to choose the words that are right for us in our mothering, to truthfully describe it, and to question and lift judgments around it as we begin to understand its complexity. This paves the way for us to value our maternal ambivalence.

When I attempt to explain maternal ambivalence to people, it becomes clear that in the majority of cases, there is a misunderstanding about the meaning of the term. This doesn't surprise me; I'm still refining it after more than ten years. Without Rozsika Parker's groundbreaking thinking, we almost certainly would not have come as far as we have in the last half century in our understanding of mothering. Parker's awareness of the myriad and conflicting feelings that compose the mother's everyday experiences, together with her insistence that maternal hating feelings have worth, has deeply influenced my perception of mothering and the value of maternal ambivalence.

Despite the high regard I have for Parker's work, I have moved away from an absolute reliance on her definition of maternal ambivalence as the mother's loving and hating feelings sitting together.

This brings me to a major dilemma with this subject: Is it okay to hate? This is the elephant in the room when we talk about ambivalence.

While I believe that Parker used the word "hatred" to disrupt and to encourage reflection and a deep and thoughtful pondering, this has not always been my experience. To this end, I have repurposed her thinking while holding firmly to her belief of the healing, redemptive forces of our disturbing emotions, which both push us to the edge and almost always bring some sort of renewal afterward. As I continue to home in on maternal ambivalence, a few main ideas are emerging for me.

While Parker focuses on love and hate in her definition of maternal ambivalence, I have noticed something missing. While she does encourage a dialogue with maternal hatred and pays attention to the rhythm of maternal ambivalence, its push and pull, there remains a lack of attention to the degree of complexity that belongs to the mother's everyday experience. Parker's definition doesn't take into account the variations and shades that exist in the mother's loving emotions, such as feelings of enjoyment, compassion, delight, and in her darker emotions, including fear, resentment, shame, guilt, despair, and abhorrence. All these sensations must be named, claimed, and given breathing space.

Any scrutiny of maternal love and hate is complex. Whereas loving feelings are most often attended by an ease of expression, the darker emotions tend to be misunderstood, neglected, or judged harshly. To take this further, linking the word "hatred" with mothering is a minefield.

However, Parker's use of "hatred" is often a distraction from the real purpose, which is a working understanding of ambivalence. We get stuck on this word. Why? There is no doubt in my mind that an admission of even small sparks of maternal hate is a scary thought. It strikes us to our core, is extremely uncomfortable, and incites passionate responses. In my own work, I can recall many instances in discussions about maternal ambivalence when the mention of that word, "hate," signaled a marked change in the atmosphere. Some people became overwhelmed, unable to contemplate the possibility. Sometimes there was a shutdown or a change of subject, often accompanied by moralizing or fury toward me. Others gave a nod of understanding and wanted to know more. These responses continue to be thought-provoking for me. The one constant is that a discussion surrounding maternal hate is never dull: it agitates. While troubling and often unwelcome, it is also irresistible. There is always curiosity, often disgust—venom. Sometimes compassion is lacking, and at other times, it is churning. All these responses are a sign that I've hit a nerve, which means that there's some truth here. To add to this, the proposition that these moments could possibly have value, the capacity to fuel and remind us of our love, and that they are an opportunity for growth and creativity seems a bit hard to fathom. It's all so contradictory and goes against what we have been taught to believe.

While society may not yet be ready to accept Parker's argument that maternal hating feelings exist, perhaps she is voicing what others cannot say. She goes out on a limb in her use of the word "hatred." She recounts that she considered other words to replace hatred, but none satisfied her. Parker soundly reasons that no other word has the power that "hatred" commands. I agree with Parker that when we avoid any words or feelings, we risk leaving out a whole area of understanding in the maternal experience. As abhorrent as it sounds, hatred is a natural, normal feeling that needs to be recognized and understood, not judged. By choosing such an extreme word, Parker established that no feelings are off-limits. This has opened a space to honestly and safely talk about many maternal feelings.

"Hate" is defined as "to regard with a strong or passionate dislike; detest."[6] While this makes sense in most relationships and exchanges, when we apply the word to mothering, we are met with disruptive and disturbing feelings. Barbara Almond, who writes about mothering and ambivalence in her book *The Monster Within: The Hidden Side of Motherhood*,[7] echoes this by reasoning that, while hating anyone besides your child renders you "unfortunate, unreasonable, bigoted, interpersonally difficult, even seriously disturbed," it can be tolerated. In contrast, she continues, "But if you hate your children, you are considered monstrous—immoral, unnatural, and evil."[8] In other words, it is acceptable to talk about hating almost anyone else, including romantic partners, parents, and neighbors, but not your child. What underlies this is that only a bad mother, a selfish witch, an ungrateful devil could possibly harbor any feelings except true, full love and self-sacrifice toward her child. This traditional and divided narrative continues to undermine the truth that the mother can hold many conflictual and dark maternal feelings and still be attentive and loving. This lies at the heart of society's hypocrisy when it comes to mothering and its refusal to entertain ideas suggestive of hatred and its role in ambivalence.

Parker's suggestion that it is acutely painful for the mother to acknowledge that "she hates where she loves"[9] has invited a lot of questions for me, while at the same time helping me to refine my own understanding of maternal hate. I have continually struggled with and asked myself: What are my own thoughts about the idea of maternal hate? What do mothers who can't bear the thought of the word "hate" do with these feelings when they surface? How can mothers straddle the reality that there is some truth in the word, but there is also social pressure and expectations to disown and silence these feelings? Why do so many mothers simply get stuck on the propriety of regarding hating feelings as the enemy rather than exploring and reflecting on them? Where does this leave the mother? Fay Weldon's words in Parker's book that "the greatest advantage of not having children must be that you can go on believing that you are a nice person"[10] are certainly worth thinking about. They hold truth. Rearing and caring for children pushes us to our limits and often leaves us raw. Let's take care not to judge our own or others' mothering.

This reminds me of my own history with the word "hatred." Until I was in my mid-thirties, I shared the more common belief of the unspeakable nature of the word. I was brought up to believe that hatred was bad, immovable, and wrong, and I didn't question this. Not until one day, when a colleague and I were discussing hatred, and he said to me, "What is so bad about hating feelings? Do they kill anyone?" It hit me: they are feelings, not actions. They are a natural part of being human and are entirely separate from the biases and beliefs that incite cruelty or violence. I felt as though a burden had been lifted—I felt freer. This conversation has allowed me to dive into the notion of maternal hatred with a fluid rather than rigid approach, with an awareness to keep my prejudices in check.

While these questions continue to baffle me, they have also helped me to shape some nonnegotiable conditions relating to the word "hatred" in the context of maternal ambivalence. I have resolved that any mention of hate is reserved to mean flashes of hatred, which is a moving dynamic, not a static state. These flickers of hate are feelings, not actions, and cannot be distinguished from the mother's love; in fact, they fuel and nourish it. To be clear, my use of hatred has no connection to brutality and atrocity, such as systemic racial torment and genocide.

There is considerable confusion surrounding the understanding of maternal ambivalence as a universal and silenced part of mothering. This lack of clarity and the confusion are not lost on me; perhaps this is not a coincidence. Ownership of maternal ambivalence is a confused and a confusing state. How do we give worth to an experience that tolerates a mother's dark feelings toward her child? Usually, when I ask people what ambivalence means, there is misunderstanding and uncertainty, a stumbling. Sometimes I hear, "Isn't ambivalence mixed feelings?" Which doesn't get close to the power of the experience. Sometimes I meet with blank stares. Then there's the most common reply: "Isn't ambivalence the same as indifference?" Which is an interesting way to understand what maternal ambivalence is emphatically not. Indifference is an absence of caring; it is a static and emotional severing. It is a disconnection. Ambivalence is a dynamic force; it ebbs and flows and is vital. While indifference paralyzes, ambivalence relies on movement, the gathering of all feelings. It has the potential for repair. There is a common misunderstanding that hatred is the polar opposite of love. I would argue, in agreement with David Mann,[11] that the opposite of love is not hate—it is indifference.[12] And for a mother, the threat is not in her fleeting moments of hatred, which force her to engage with her feelings. The danger is indifference; this is the enemy. I saw an experience of maternal indifference being played out before me that has stayed with me. It took place at a prize-giving ceremony many years ago, where a community benefactor who was estranged from her son was attending the event. As he climbed the stage time after time to receive his accolades, her face and eyes betrayed an emptiness, absolutely no acknowledgement, no flicker of pride or love or even hatred. In those moments I witnessed the shocking power of indifference—a cutting off.

This blurring of indifference and ambivalence is particularly concerning because it undermines the central role that ambivalence holds in the maternal language as a fluid and healing dynamic. It is crucial to disengage these terms from each other. What I find peculiar is that indifference, this not-caring, this cutting off, is often more acceptable than an admission of strong, dark feelings, including moments of hate. How can indifference with its core of disconnection be regarded as a more socially acceptable emotion than hate with its movement and possibility for transformation and repair? I think this returns to our cultural standards, which favor maintaining taboo rather than fostering an openness and conversation about abhorrent maternal feelings.

It is vitally important to safeguard a space for moms to be courageous and self-aware of their truths and to name them, even moments of hate, as we explore and learn from them. Let's be curious rather than judgmental. For some mothers, any censoring of the word "hate" may be received as a message that these feelings are odious, and as an extension of this, that she doesn't have the right to the full feelings that comprise her mothering. This limits the safe and productive places available for her to understand all her real feelings, which may lead to her judging herself, feeling ashamed, and tending to minimize and ignore her truth. This is not a good space for a mother to inhabit. As a society, we need to face the fact that mothering incites a diverse range of feelings, including dark and troublesome ones, and if we silence any of these moments, we miss an entire area of a mother's experience and deny a significant part of the maternal language.

This brings me to the significance I place on finding the right words as a way to understand our lived experience. As maternal thinkers, it is our task to develop an understanding about the layers of meaning and feeling that are attached to words. A mother's perception of her emotions is wholly subjective, and we need to free ourselves to use any words that are fit for her to claim and describe her feelings. Of course, we don't all experience our feelings in the same way or have the same words to describe them, but if we censor and avoid words, then we are leaving out a whole area of understanding in the maternal experience. As abhorrent as it sounds, it is a natural, normal feeling that needs to be recognized and understood, not judged. This reasoning informs my understanding of mothering and maternal ambivalence.

What one mother may call "anguish" will be "upset" to another, and these feelings can fluctuate from minute to minute. A mother often experiences a cluster of many different feelings at any one time. These may include resentment, anger, tenderness, love, fear, loss, loneliness, boredom, pain, anguish, and devotion. My undertaking is to encourage mothers to name and own their own feelings with honesty and without judgment, to limit self-shame and blame and bring in self-forgiveness. Naming a feeling gives it meaning and makes it real.

When we discover a descriptive word or a phrase that echoes our lived experience, we undergo transformation, a *wow* moment. A descriptive word or phrase speaks to us; we are in rhythm with it. It helps us to claim our experience. It's a relief; it helps us feel whole. Naming an experience also contributes to normalizing it. Once a word is spoken, it is granted a place as well as permission to expand on feelings around it. It humanizes the experience. When I first glanced at Parker's book on maternal ambivalence, I experienced such a moment. I was enthralled by the word "ambivalence." I kind of knew what it meant but wasn't really sure whether I really understood it. The definition, "the co-existence in one person of opposite or conflicting feelings towards someone or something," grabbed me. I identified with it; it made complete sense to me. By applying the concept of ambivalence to mothering, the pieces of the jigsaw fell into place. It allows for all the different feelings that a mother experiences. This is mothering.

My own struggle with how to describe maternal ambivalence and to incorporate it into my work as well as my life is perhaps best exemplified in a conversation I had with my niece, the mother of four children, both teenagers and young adults. She said it so succinctly: "We all as moms have our own words for our own feelings; they belong to us." (She, who minces no words, may also have been warning me not to put words in her mouth.) Then she told me that she finds maternal ambivalence constantly in the countless everyday interactions with her children. This is the jewel for her. Now she can identify her feelings, a conflicting and puzzling array of sensations that surprise, shock, confuse, and renew her. They allow her to keep showing up. They allow her to achieve her love. These are her melting moments, when her distressing feelings, whether she knows them as anger, resentment, pity, loneliness, or even flashes of hate, meet with her love. These moments signal maternal ambivalence.

TWO

THE PARADOX OF MOTHERHOOD

ONE OF THE KEYS TO managing everyday life as a mom is learning to lean into the reality that motherhood is the ultimate paradox, "a statement or proposition seemingly self-contradictory or absurd, and yet explicable as expressing a truth."[13] Mothering is strange; it can be confusing and confronting, it brings us to our truth, and more often than not, it contains elements of the unexpected. From its first moments, birth plans and breastfeeding are guaranteed to go awry. The terrible twos last for more like five years; teenage behavior causes untold heartbreak. The daily minutiae of pre-dawn wake-up, picky food phases, rainy-day boredom, tantrums, schoolwork, and everything in between provokes a range of emotions (and exhaustion) from joy and euphoria to anger, impatience, and self-hatred.

Let's start with the universal paradox: almost every mother dedicates years of her life to raising her child and then becomes the one who is there to be left. While we might resent the idea or reel from it, the wise words of child psychologist Erna Furman,[14] that a mother "is there to be left,"[15] are a piercing reminder of our job. It captures the essence of so much that is true about mothering. It is contradictory, it is insightful, and it can even be empowering if we take it in the spirit that Furman intended. Let's think about what these words mean—that as mothers we are expected to be available for our child with the partly concealed knowledge that at some point in the future, this will all change. Our child will need to leave us, both psychologically and physically. Not fully, but enough—that's the jolt. This is challenging. Whether we choose to acknowledge it or remain blissfully unaware, the reality is that we will all be left by our kids one day, which is right. It's our job to stay engaged in the present—to show up every day, do the best we can, and somehow understand this process. I caution against seeing it as an abandonment, a rupture or disconnection; rather, it is a change of focus, a shift, as we move from the central role in our child's life to one on the sidelines, be it a self-interested or overly invested one.

To say it in another way, this is the push and pull of mothering—the ambivalence, the conflicts we continually feel as moms. There are times as moms we are so ready to have our own lives back again, to be child-free, but this wish is tinged with a familiar feeling of dread, a sting. We understand that our child's growth brings with it a movement away from us that can be difficult for any mother to bear. A mother finds herself adjusting continually as her child gets older and his or her needs fluctuate. Even as a teenager, the youngster will desperately rely on her mother one minute and become dismissive of her the next. A mother is expected to adjust to these ebbs and flows effortlessly, without reacting or changing her behavior toward her child. She is meant to remain consistent and reliable. She is responsible for balancing her own needs with those of her child and negotiating the right amount of emotional and physical distance between the two of them. This is a huge ask, which also leaves many questions unanswered: Where are the boundaries? When is a mother too close, and when is she too distant from her child? How does she keep up with her child's physical and emotional state while maintaining her own emotional equilibrium? And whose needs matter most: the child's, the mother's, or both? A child is vulnerable, innocent, and needy, and yet a mother puts her heart, soul, and immeasurable hours into raising her offspring so she can be there to be left. How does one make sense of this paradox? In theory, it holds no logic, but in reality, it is simply the practice of motherhood. A mother's job is to raise her child with love and nourishment, to ready her so she is able to leave and go out into the world.

How does any mother learn to manage, much less understand, this complicated and shifting dynamic? Let's think about the stages of motherhood and the demands on a mother from her point of view. It begins with the child's initial, and almost complete physical and emotional, dependency on the mother. (Some might argue that it begins even before birth, with the emotional or hormonal inward cry to conceive a baby.) Her life is dictated by and supposedly in tune with the mood and presence of her baby. Each day revolves around meeting her infant's needs and the constant juggling that feeding, settling, and holding requires. Balancing the demands of her infant, herself, the rest of her family, and the outside world is both agony and ecstasy. Love, care, and compassion, tossed together with turmoil, weariness, and worry, signal that life is no longer her own. Any former freedom is replaced by full responsibility for another human being.

There are instances of peace and solace when a contented or tired baby sleeps, and loving moments spent bathing and caressing, talking tenderly, and singing songs, as the baby gazes at her and eventually responds with babbles and smiles. Then there are the other moments of bewilderment, uncertainty, tension, and fatigue when the baby cannot sleep or is continually crying, as an exhausted mother tries to find out what the problem is, asking many questions—of doctors, of their own mothers, even of the baby who can't yet answer. Sometimes cuddling and rocking works, and sometimes it doesn't. The mother wonders whether her baby has a tummy ache, is hungry, or is overtired, or whether something is really wrong. At some point, most mothers wonder whether they are spoiling their baby by picking her up or holding her too often. What if the baby never learns to self-soothe? And yet, what if she just needs to be hugged and comforted?

For some mothers, this period is more fraught than it is for others. This is a complicated time, and a mother is affected by many experiences, including past traumas, her partnership or marriage, her current social and economic situation, or recuperation from a difficult pregnancy or birth. These factors and others all play a role in how she connects with her infant. For most mothers, the reality is that these early days of absolute dependence are turbulent. A mother sways between small, effortless routines that are almost automatic, like changing a diaper, and much more volatile moments that require concentration and tenacity: holding her baby during a vaccination or trying to settle a screaming infant. There are hardly words for the exhaustion, powerlessness, and wonder that this time of motherhood provokes.

This stage of the mother's total dedication to her infant isn't without its complexity. While the mother-child relationship appears to be one in which the infant has total dependence on the mother, this is a mutual process for both. The mother is usually contentedly oblivious that she'll become the one who will be left. Subtle hints are present from the early days, which can warn the mother of her child's future movement away from her. In her book *Maternal Encounters*,[16] Lisa Baraitser, a contemporary thinker and writer, tackles mothering as a shocking experience that brings disarray, interruption, and separateness together with the chance for renewal. Baraitser reflects on how a child's experience of falling asleep can be a symbol of his separateness, a delicate shifting away from his mother. Baraitser recalls in heartfelt terms how watching her child falling asleep once brought tears to her eyes as she saw him "removed to a place where she couldn't go with him....She watched as the child turned away."[17] This marked a moment of both emotional turmoil and renewal, as Baraitser experienced a surging of deep maternal love with a realization that her child wasn't hers to keep.

The intense mutual reliance of the early months lessens over time, as the mother and her child make mutual adjustments to and for each other. This is rarely smooth sailing, as the mother and her child have many clashing desires and needs. Conflicts, contradictions, and paradoxes surface, and reverse steps are often the order of the day. As the adult, a mother must learn to continually contract and expand her presence according to her understanding of her child's needs in any given moment. A dance of closeness and distance unfolds as the child's search for independence is matched with a need to return to her over and over again. At each stage of her child's life, a mother's job is to emotionally and physically manage these shifts and the growth towards and away from her. As the child begins to crawl, walk, and talk, he begins to venture away from his mother with the confidence that she is a safe beacon who is always there to return to. But this is a practice run, and in the end, as he reaches adulthood, while he may return temporarily during periods of vulnerability, his true growth as an adult relies on a healthy distance between them. While the mother is aware that her child will grow up and that she must surrender this part of her life, it is still often jarring for her to accept this reality. In acknowledging this, and recognizing herself, who in Furman's words is the "one who is there to be left,"[18] the mother gives a gift of freedom to her child, to herself, and to the likelihood of a new, healthy, and more adult relationship between them.

I often think being a mother is like being an accordion player. She holds her child in her hands, stretching, contracting, and releasing her grip. On a physical and emotional level, her self-awareness and flexibility mean that she never fully releases her child. The mother leads and follows, learns from and teaches, while letting go and holding on. It's certainly not easy to get this rhythm right. A mother needs to develop an understanding of when she is actually needed and when she needs to be in waiting, to be aware of not interfering in her child's life. While letting go has many false starts and conflicts, the mother's light-bulb moment, that her child is not hers but his own person, can be a stark, if obvious, realization.

There is the universal story of a stay-at-home mother leaving her child on the first day of preschool. Her heart is pounding. Strong feelings of loss become a lump in her throat as she says to herself, "Lucy is not ready for this," knowing that really she's the one who isn't ready to let go. Emotions contract and expand as she fights the desire to take her daughter back home. Instead, she says goodbye, and then waits at the nearby coffee shop for a phone call from the school, just in case, which doesn't come. She thinks about what her own life holds now that she is home alone between 9 a.m. and 3 p.m. (Even mothers who eagerly look forward to finally having time to themselves after several years of 24/7 childcare find it difficult at first to fill the suddenly empty hours.) She doesn't want to let her own fears overwhelm and limit her daughter, but she cannot wait until she picks Lucy up again in the afternoon. It's a long day of loss. When she collects Lucy, the little girl is tired, excited, and happy to go home with her mother. They will both adapt to their new rhythm in a few days, but these feelings stay with the mother.

The story above reflects the mothering structure that our society has also helped to put in place, though the push and pull of a child's need for independence comes from within too. Trevor is eight years old and has been nagging his mom to let him walk to the store a mile down the street. Sherry is reluctant because when she was the same age, a friend of hers was hit by a car when she crossed the road at her first outing. To make things worse, Trevor wants to take his six-year-old sister Jess with him. Sherry is bewildered and uncertain as her own childhood memories come flooding back, and she is having difficulty separating her own experiences from those of her child. There's safety in numbers, but they are both her children. She thinks, "Maybe I'll let them go and drive behind," but she quickly gathers herself. She knows she's lost this one, and part of her knows Trevor is right. But she makes the right decision for him and for her younger child, saying, "It's so good of you to offer to take your sister, but I'm not quite ready for you both to go, so why don't you call Jeff to see if he can go with you?" Trevor calls and they make the plan to meet outside in fifteen minutes. Sherry has butterflies in her stomach, but she has to let him go and trust that he will be okay, armed with a mobile phone and instructions to call when he arrives. On his return an hour later, he looks more grown up, with a big smile on his face and a chocolate for Jess. What a thoughtful brother he is. Sherry knows of course that this trip is the beginning of future demands for more independence. She realizes how closely connected his desire for autonomy is with her wish to hold him back. She is hit by the irony of this, understanding that it's an illusion to believe that she can control, and thereby protect, her child forever. Mothering teaches the rawest life lesson: the only control you have is in surrendering to the reality that control doesn't really exist. By changing her mindset, Sherry is able to claw back a bit of her agency.

Football aptly illustrates this particular movement toward independence in the mother-child relationship. The goalposts move, and Mom shifts from center field to the sidelines as her child becomes a teenager. She cheers her child from the perimeter, being mindful not to step onto the field. Her job description is different now. She can provide oranges, drinks, and sweets when her child reaches out for them, though he doesn't always come to her outstretched arms. Furman advises that a mother cannot afford to be upset about this and that she needs to have her own purposeful life outside of her child's ball game. She will still be desperately needed at times, and at others she is bound to feel discarded. Learning to cope with this allows a mother to sense her child's love anew, albeit in a different way.

Let's not forget the time when the child leaves home. The mother is so close to her daughter; she is overjoyed that she's moving in with her boyfriend, but she is also so sad. She will miss their talks, their years of cooking together, laughing, and companionship. The daughter ends up moving five minutes away, and when she looks outside, she can see her grandmother's house in the distance—the chains of mothering over the generations are maintained.

It's the lifelong struggle of motherhood, a constant coming to terms with the reality that as a mother, your job is to be "always available so as not to be needed, always there to be left, always to bear the pain and anger at being inevitably rejected, and in the grateful, luminous moments, to feel the bittersweet joy of your children's ever-growing independence and love of life."[19]

While Furman's ideas are helpful as a guide and a baseline for mothers to understand as they grow and evolve into a healthy and (all things being relative) happy motherhood, the multiple paradoxes that unfold can be bewildering. Sometimes the dance of closeness and distance has an easy rhythm to it, as she holds onto and releases her child, often simultaneously, and at other times, a mother feels entirely out of sync. The continual contractions and expansions—which of course begin during pregnancy, as the woman makes room for the new being growing inside, and the experience of labor—all hint toward our future lives as mothers. While few of us register this at the time, we are soon set straight by our child.

Then there are struggles connected with the mother realizing that her child's body belongs to him not her, a loss in which a mother must release her "conscious or unconscious investment of her child as part of her own body."[20] Examples include a mother's arguments with her teenage daughter about the clothes she wants to wear or the overnight stays at her boyfriend's house; today, the battle rages with nearly every child over getting a tattoo. A mother has to learn to choose her battles well, adapting sometimes and at other times refusing to give in to her child's demands, as she develops a recognition that her child's ultimate independence paradoxically relies on a period of initial dependence and that this doesn't necessarily move in a straight line. It's a roller coaster.

Above all, a mother needs to cultivate the ability to communicate honestly, lovingly, and consistently with her child as she or he grows up. That process begins with a mother's recognition of her own inner landscape and in developing a certain fluency in the language of maternal ambivalence. Just as we help teach our children how to speak to us, how to advocate for their needs, mothers need to do the same.

There's no road map for our important mission as creators of our children's independence. This lifelong dance between mother and child spans the mothering experience. It prompts many questions, and if approached with mindfulness, we have the opportunity to ask ourselves some or all of them again and again throughout our lives.

How do we as mothers work with our feelings about being left?

What do we do with this truth?

How do we find the words to prepare us to help our child to leave?

How do we create the capacity, or adult maturity, to manage our personal feelings about being left?

How can we process smoldering feelings of rejection when we are "left"?

How do we balance motherhood versus personhood, forging a new path with agency when life is no longer centered upon children?

How do we avoid seeing ourselves as "objects" and the resentment that comes along with it?

Take a moment to formulate your own questions. Write them down, and revisit or update them periodically, observing the shifts in your mood and self-awareness over time. It takes trial and error for every mother to find her own healthy sense of equilibrium. If we can reconcile the idea that the pain of our loss is secondary to our child's progress, then we are more likely to participate in his growth rather than interfere with it. And, when we learn to get creative with the painful feelings we hold about our child's independence, we can discover that there are many wonderful opportunities for us to experience our own growth as our children move away from us. Furthermore, by accepting our child's expressions of independence and the parallel feelings of loss that we experience, we can learn self-compassion and forgive them for what is natural and largely healthy behavior. These ebbs and flows move between a full preoccupation in the early years to a more dormant experience in later years, when the mother remains in constant, unconscious vigilance in case she is ever needed. Whether our child is newborn or fifty years old, we're still on the sidelines, or on the backfoot, lagging behind them. Sometimes they want and need us, and at other times they don't. This is our lesson. As the mother begins to seize back a little of her independence, she is nonetheless always ready to "serve" her child's needs when necessary. Furman aptly describes this dynamic in which the mother allows herself "to miss her child, to feel not needed, and to remain lovingly available for the moments when he chooses to return to her."[21] This is motherhood.

The mother often struggles to recover her agency to effect healthy change and competence within herself. This demands that she reclaim parts of herself, notably her individuality, her purpose, and her ability to make healthy decisions for herself separate from that of her child: capacities that may well have been compromised, forgotten, or put to the side during years of hands-on child-rearing. This requires a reset both for herself and with how she thinks about her child. When she is fluid rather than rigid, she is then more able to be generous, forgiving, and hopeful for the future. Any use of power, guilt, or blame is a no-no. To build up her agency, the mother will lean into her inner feelings, which are often contradictory, including her losses, fears, and pains. Her relationship with her child will be based on mutual acceptance, not expectation. These faculties are often marked at a later stage when the child is able to show compassion and understanding toward his mother as an individual, as he can "thank her at times and increasingly show...concern for her."[22] Even as our maternal agency thrives, we still yearn to be appreciated and noticed by our child, however separate this becomes to achieving our well-being.

The 2017 film *Lady Bird*[23] tells a familiar coming-of-age story that illustrates the paradox of the mother who knows on one level that she needs to let her child go while at the same time she consciously, and unconsciously, tries to sabotage her daughter's independence. Seventeen-year-old Lady Bird and her mother, Marion McPherson, experience the typical swing between arguments and affection that most teenagers and their mothers encounter. The plot traces Lady Bird's journey through her last year of high school in Sacramento, California, as she struggles with fights with friends, her first sexual encounter, and persistent battles and reconciliations with her mother about clothes, the way she walks, her newly adopted name "Lady Bird," her school grades, the family's financial pressures, and notably her decision about which college she will attend. The film depicts the age-old mother-and-teenage-child struggle and the internal push and pull that mothers experience as they first resist reality and then eventually come to terms with the knowledge that they are the one who is there to be left, all while balancing their own and their child's clashing needs for closeness and distance. Marion's difficulty in letting go of Lady Bird as she plans on leaving home is acted out in their fights about which college the girl should attend. Marion tries to undermine Lady Bird's attempts to apply to a prestigious out-of-state school, a prospect that provokes layers of maternal anxiety for Marion, who fears that with the distance she may lose her daughter forever, especially if Lady Bird finds a better life there.

Lady Bird echoes Furman's ideas about the maternal struggles with contradictory feelings that surface as one's child grows up and moves away. One of the most moving scenes in the film unfolds when it is revealed that Lady Bird has secretly applied to an out-of-state college with her father's approval. When Marion discovers this betrayal, she refuses to speak to Lady Bird and ignores her daughter's pleas for forgiveness. It's a heartbreaking reaction, if an understandable one, and a scenario to learn from: the mother who uses physical or emotional methods to impede or block the process of separation only invites more unhappiness for herself and her child. Marion struggles to understand that Lady Bird is separate from her, which marks the difficulties that often accompany a mother's "transfer of body ownership," the acceptance that her child needs the freedom to grow away from her. It seems that for Marion, Lady Bird is an extension of herself, so the girl must abide by her wishes—for example, by attending a school that Marion approves of and living her life in a certain way. When Lady Bird rejects these demands, Marion is forced to surrender and accept that the former closeness with her child, which in some way functioned to hold her together, is now lost. As Furman writes in the example of a mother and son, this part that the mother loses "has become a part of him and ceased to be hers."[24] Marion must decide how she will react to this, and in the early stages, she cuts her daughter out. She is stuck in her pain and anger and is not able to replenish herself. Paradoxically, as Lady Bird prepares to leave home after gaining entry to her first-choice college, she quickly becomes independent. In the temporary absence of her relationship with her mother, Lady Bird gets a job, a driver's license, and cleans and paints her room, which demonstrates how well our children can do when they are left to their own devices. During this time, there is almost a mother-daughter role reversal, as Marion becomes nearly paralyzed in her extreme psychic pain. She is unable to soothe herself or to return to being an adult, much less to achieve agency for herself. In a poignant moment, she tries unsuccessfully to find the right words to write to Lady Bird, seated at a table surrounded by many crumpled pieces of paper.

Toward the end, there is a profoundly painful scene as Marion is unable to say farewell to Lady Bird at the airport as the girl leaves for college. She drops Lady Bird at the curbside with her father, refusing to park in a garage, using the excuse that it is too expensive and that they cannot go to the airline gate anyway. When Marion realizes her mistake and collapses into tears of grief, she quickly parks the car, runs through the airport, and discovers that she is too late. This is a familiar maternal feeling that most mothers are able to identify with: a feeling of lost opportunity. Marion breaks down as she understands that she's sacrificed the chance to say farewell to her daughter in a fitting way as she starts a new phase of her life. Marion is inconsolable as she recognizes the part she has played in the drama. She can no longer avoid the reality that she is the one who is there to be left. There are also changes in store for Lady Bird. When the girl arrives at college, she experiences a new reality. After getting drunk at a party and ending up in the hospital, she calls her mother, who isn't there to answer the phone, and leaves her a lovely message of hope and forgiveness. The child who has retreated from her mother rediscovers her need for her parent and is equally able to thank her with newfound compassion and love.

While we're left wondering how Marion will respond to Lady Bird's message, Furman's heartfelt and universal words about children returning home come to mind. "It even continues after the children have moved out to work or study away from home, when every effort is made to keep ready a sleeping space, a special meal, and a warm welcome, and it sometimes shows in tears at a child's wedding."[25]

Marion is an embodiment of the unanswered questions I've noted above that so many mothers ask themselves over the years and, for mothers of any age, the process by which to begin repairing the effects of so many conflicting feelings that cause untold pain for themselves and their children. Is a mother stuck in her own feelings of anger and hurt, or can she achieve a sense of agency and purpose even as she preserves a symbolic space in her heart and her home for when her child chooses to return? These monumental challenges require every mother to gather all of her adult capabilities to navigate this bittersweet process and the losses and gains that mark her emotional and physical movements toward and away from her child.

LOSING AND FINDING

Then there's the paradox that mother and child continually lose and find each other in their search for physical and emotional connection. Every mother is entrusted with holding the tension that surfaces as she and her child discover and learn from and about each other, as she continually claims and reclaims her child, and a circular flow is set up between them. Mom is responsible for shielding her children from that outright aggression or pain that their development incurs, while paving the way for them to learn to acknowledge and process feelings for themselves. As part of that dynamic, mothers and children shift between losing and finding each other. Gill Rye, a professor and writer who has done prolific research on mothering, makes one of the most profound statements about mothering that I have encountered, in her book *Narratives of Mothering*:[26] "Loss—or the fear or fantasy of loss—is at the very heart of the mothering experience."[27] These words have reframed how I approach mothering, as continual experiences of losses and adjustments to them. By naming an experience clearly as a loss, however, there must be a flip side—an opportunity to find something. Another paradox sits inside this one as the mother is constantly in a mirror process of losing and finding herself. Mothering is a lifelong experience of continually claiming and reclaiming, losing and finding the baby, toddler, child, teenager, and the young and not-so-young adult. In the losing, the mother experiences a renewal and a change as she seeks to find her child, and when her expectations shift, she may find her child a different person from the one she had imagined.

One of the earliest and most powerful demonstrations of the mother and child losing and finding each other is often also the most terribly fraught: the early weeks or months of feeding. A mother prepares a safe, comfortable space to ensure the best opportunity for the baby to find her food and a connection with her mother. At this stage of infanthood, milk represents nourishment, warmth, and security. When it flows, there is satisfaction (physical and psychological) and connection; the baby is full and content. But when the stars don't align—and on many occasions they don't—the infant resists the food. The ensuing distress and disturbance means the connection at this point is lost between them. This prompts every mother to search for answers: Is the temperature right? Is the formula fresh? Did I eat something wrong today that has upset her? Does my baby have a tummy ache? Am I holding the bottle at the right angle? Is the milk coming too fast or slow? Do I need to change the diaper?

In most cases, the mother identifies the problem, the feed is restored, and the mother and baby find each other. She makes sure that the baby is latching onto her breast or a bottle and that her breathing isn't blocked. If the baby is screaming, squirming, and whining, the connection is momentarily lost; they both focus on finding it through the milk. The mother may try expressing some of her breast milk or formula onto her finger and then rubbing it gently inside her infant's mouth. The taste of the milk usually soothes the baby and coaxes him to latch onto the breast or take the teat. In most instances, the mother works out a way for them to find each other. The mother learns about her infant through the contented faces he makes, including reflex smiles and wavering eyelids that follow a good feed. In both bottle and breast, when the feed is complete and the baby is satisfied, the mother has had an experience of finding an emotional connection between her baby and herself.

But most of us know that feeding a baby—in any way—can at times be a painstaking, heartbreaking task, even if a short-lived one. Finding each other can be difficult sometimes. As long as it happens enough of the time, a mother can feel confident and able to establish a connection with her infant, and her baby will feel claimed. So many raw life lessons unfold as a mother continually loses and finds her child.

Losing and finding one's child is a journey of discovery and a constant struggle. It is so tremendously important that these dynamics unfold in a stable yet fluid atmosphere for both mother and child. This requires the mother's self-awareness and ability to recognize, repair, and learn from her mistakes without judging herself or her child.

A patient, whom I'll call Rose, recounted a story to me almost a year after our lives had been turned upside down by the global pandemic. Her daughter reminded her every day that her birthday party the previous year in New York had been cancelled because of COVID. This one, she was told, needed to be bigger and better.

"Bigger?" she said to me. "Two things crossed my mind: she has fewer friends since we've moved three times in eighteen months, and...we're still in the middle of a pandemic!"

I asked her how she was planning to manage her daughter's expectations. Rose's reply: "I desperately wanted to give it a shot! We have a new backyard in our house in California, so I knew we could have a bit of fun. The theme was Candy Land, and I invited literally everyone I knew. I ordered the biggest bounce house I could find (a gingerbread house, of course). I scattered inflatable man-sized candy canes, lollipops, and gobstoppers around the lawn—yes, I blew them up myself! I borrowed tables and chairs and found bright-red table linens for a pop. Plates, napkins, balloons, and party favors were all in theme and personalized. Even the cake was an explosion of candy and color. Pure drama, bigger and better everywhere you looked.

"My daughter had a blast—until the last guest left, and then she cried and cried and cried. 'Why the tears? It was perfect! You had so much fun!' I kept saying. But nothing I said could break her sadness. The rest of the day she was miserable. She didn't like the theme, apparently no one played with her (except they all did!), the music was too babyish, she didn't like her cake, and the presents weren't great either.

"I'd poured my heart and soul into making this birthday one she would never forget. Instead of running to me with open arms, saying, 'Thank you, Mommy,' I was being told it was the worst day ever. After my initial confusion, rage kicked in. 'You selfish, ungrateful, spoiled brat! This behavior is ridiculous. Do you know how many kids would give the world to have a party like this? You don't deserve any of this!' I used so many adjectives to describe her, as she cried even harder. I left her to cry. She wailed and wailed. I was reeling, especially because I could have given the money to some other kid who really needed it or cared. She just didn't understand!"

Rose was nearly in tears herself while describing the scene to me. She went on: "Weeks have now passed...last night we were looking for a book to read and came across her yearbook from her previous school in New York. As we looked at it together in bed, a wave of emotion came over her, and she started sobbing. And she cried and cried and cried. She hadn't cried like this since her party. It took her a while to utter three words: 'I...miss...my...' My heart sank. And it suddenly dawned on me. As perfect as the party seemed, it wasn't perfect at all. It was filled with so many friendly faces, but to her it was empty.

"I didn't need to hear the rest of her sentence. She misses so much. Her friends, her family, her life before. All this time, it was me. I was the one who didn't understand."

Rose's story is a reminder that we all need, and yearn for, the right environment in which to interact, to accept, and to grow. I use the word "fluid" above, but others might describe it as mindful, peaceful, stable, calm, open-minded, or open-hearted. As mothers, we're always looking for a way to soothe or fulfill our children's wishes and desires, though they're not always adept at expressing them accurately. Giving ourselves the space to communicate gently yet consistently with our child allows us to find them again and again more easily, and allows us to forgive ourselves and to be kinder and gentler with ourselves when we miss the mark, which inevitably happens again and again.

Then there is Prue's story. She and her sixteen-year-old son, Sam, had previously enjoyed a happy, communicative relationship, losing and finding each other with relative ease. As his teenage years began, things hit a snag, culminating in a tough reckoning for them both. Sam went out one night with classmates who all had driver's licenses, though he hadn't gotten one yet, being younger than them. When he returned at midnight, Prue saw him get out of the driver's seat, and she was furious. The many thoughts, feelings, and fears collided in her head. What if he'd had an accident and hurt himself or someone else? She'd talked about this with him so many times, and now he had gone and done it behind her back. Her first thought was that she should have held him back at school so he would be with kids his own age. It was just irresponsible, on both of their parts.

When Sam came in, Prue said all of these things and more. Sam's usually bright eyes became dim; after briefly saying sorry, he retreated to his bedroom. Prue was aghast. She'd blown this one, missing an opportunity for discussion and finding out why he'd done it instead of a barrage of criticism. Her fear was justified; things could have really gone wrong. But she had lost him emotionally with her rigidity.

The next morning, Prue felt ready to open the conversation. Sam was polite, but his eyes wouldn't meet her gaze. This went on for a few more days, and Prue started to feel desperate. There was nothing worse than this silence, this icy air, as she thought, "I was too tough on him. Maybe I needed to listen." She realized that he was no longer a child. Losing Sam was painful, but she would need to bear this until he came around, and she had to trust that a reconciliation would happen—a hope and an unknown.

It did. But it took another week. Prue had to contain herself as she listened to her son explain that he'd had a hard night with his friends. He had done the wrong thing by driving, but he needed some understanding, not recrimination, from her.

He explained that he'd needed time to work out his anger and frustration and that he really knew that during the previous few weeks she'd remained there for him, despite his silence. They found each other again. Both learned a lesson. Prue learned that as a mother she had to be there waiting for him to come back on his terms, to be found, and that a shift in the relationship was occurring. She had to find a way to reconnect and construct a new language for their connection. She somehow knew that their way forward would involve losing and finding each other as he grew to adulthood, and she accepted this new cycle. In maintaining her presence, they found a reboot and a renewal that would be repeated many times.

Each of these stories illustrates that mothering is a process of making mistakes and learning from them, and of checking our expectations continually. A mother of an infant understands on some level that feeding is connection. Sometimes the feed goes to plan; others require her to find her infant again despite the difficulty and to understand that her job is to hold herself and her infant "enough" of the time to sustain the losses and to keep moving forward together. This means creating a safe, reliable space in which a mother can keep learning about herself and her child. Rose was burdened by her own rigid expectations and her fury at her daughter's lack of gratitude. They lost each other. Her daughter's ability to express her feelings openly a few nights later and Rose's ability to understand the message her daughter was communicating created a crucial reconnection for them. It is also a startling reminder of a mother's responsibility to hold the tension between them with awareness and the possibility that a gift of new understanding, learning, and finding gives. Prue was able to understand that a new relationship was unfolding with her son. Her job was to recognize this and to use the silence between them, a temporary loss, as an opportunity to support, to listen rather than speak, and to wait, as she held the space between them and learned from this experience.

The very existence of this contradiction or tension between losing and finding is both a warning bell and an anchor for a mother, alerting her to listen to her child and to be attuned to each of their sensitivities while refraining from judgment. One loss becomes an opportunity for rediscovery.

MOTHERING IS A MESSY, INTERRUPTED EXPERIENCE.

One of the most distressing and annoying parts of motherhood is the constant interruptions that it brings. A contradiction lies here because the interruption literally stops us in our tracks, and by throwing us off course, it forces us to rethink and perhaps change our direction. While annoying, these breaks can equally be understood as bridges that offer a mother valuable thinking space. In pressing the pause button, flow and growth come rushing in.

Interruptions in motherhood come in forms large and small—sometimes very small, sometimes very, very big. One of the largest and usually most welcomed interruptions that figures strongly for mothers is bringing a newborn home. This is accompanied by smaller and not so welcome ones: being unable to finish a cup of coffee, to have a shower, or to make a phone call without being interrupted by your baby. These interruptions don't seem so small at the time. Other interruptions include sending your child back to school after a long summer vacation at 8 a.m. and then getting a call at 9 a.m. "Mom, I forgot my sports clothes, can you please bring them to school for me now?" There are constant interruptions to work schedules. A topical interruption is sitting down to dinner with a friend for the first time after the two-year pandemic and receiving the unwelcome call: "Mom, please come home. I'm scared to be alone." Interruption is a word that encompasses all the everyday and seemingly irritating parts of motherhood, but there is more to them—let's not underestimate their value.

Baraitser describes an interruption as a kind of gap that allows for the meeting of thought, feeling, and meaning, and insists that the notion needs to be better understood rather than dismissed. By reframing and expanding this idea, Baraitser encourages us to see interruption beyond its function as an irritant and to understand it as a valuable and meaningful part of mothering. Her compelling argument considers interruptions as moments in which the mother is constantly turning herself towards her child—"mid-sentence, mid-mouthful, mid-thought, or in the middle of the night" as "she often makes herself available without finishing the things that replenish her,"[28] an experience familiar to all mothers.

So how are these instances more than just irritations and inconveniences to a mother's daily experience? Baraitser reimagines them in a novel way as an opportunity for renewal rather than as an impediment. On a meta level, pregnancy, birth, and child-rearing overtake and interrupt the mother's life in the rawest and most fundamental way, while offering her rebirth and regeneration. Then there are the familiar, mundane interruptions, the kind Baraitser describes that "trip us up, or throw us 'off the subject,'"[29] which are also a reminder of the depth of certain sensations, such as "sound, smell, emotions…"[30] I remember, myself, the times that my children's bubble bath overflowed all over the bathroom floor when the running tap was forgotten. While this meant an extra chore, cleaning the floor with lots of dry towels, this slippery, messy interruption was much more. It now carries powerful memories of joy as the children squashed the soft, sweet-scented foamy bubbles into their chubby hands and spread them onto their own and each other's bodies. The sounds of laughter, the children's splashing waves, and the smell of the bubble bath remain. Leaning into the interruption and enjoying the messiness of the moment, while counterintuitive on one level, is also an opportunity for connection, as one remains present within the interruption and feels its power.

These interruptions can provide the mother with a thinking place, a pause, if they capture her attention. They stop and startle her, and paradoxically, these "depleting, exhausting, disabling and controlling" experiences[31] can also rejuvenate her because they compel her to think and feel in a new way. However, her ability to think requires her to be fluid rather than to block off painful feelings that are incited in the interruption—reacting too quickly or negatively, or resisting by ignoring it all, invites flared tempers, heightened drama, and a near-guaranteed unhappy outcome.

A child's cry is an example of interruption. It pierces a mother's experience and stops her in her tracks, but her measured and calm acceptance of it, her flow, allows her the opportunity to shape a space to reflect, react, and transform. That cry is so much more than an emission of sound between mother and child. It's a historically charged and complicated experience for both, who have unique memories of how their cries have been managed in the past as well as their shared experience. Baraitser describes the interruption and impact of a child's cry on the mother: "We hear an infant cry: our heart rate goes up, and we get sweaty. That much at least is official."[32] This stimulates a sense of frenzy for her. At this point, the mother is faced with a range of deep feelings—panic, compassion, despair, pity, annoyance, anger, and love. If the mother is able to shape her thinking space, she can reorient an experience that stuns and paralyzes her to be one that is "enlivening and productive."[33]

Let's use the example of an interruption that disrupts the everyday morning rush before school. The morning is so far going well, and Lynn is as usual making breakfast and school lunches while mentally preparing for her day. She is going through the list in her head: "Get the kids to the bus stop on time, do the laundry by ten a.m., then I'll be able to fit in the work Zoom session before the baby wakes up at eleven-thirty, then there's time to take her to the park and to the supermarket before I—" Suddenly, she hears a bang and a shriek, and her thoughts scatter immediately. Chevy has spilled milk all over Greg's homework project and her clothes, and she is hysterical because now she has to get changed before school, and she knows Greg has been working on this for weeks, and Greg is just speechless...

This is interruption for Lynn. Before the dropping of the milk, she is absorbed in her thoughts and hopes of getting through her day seamlessly. Then she is disturbed. The question is whether she can use the interruption as a tool to gather herself and her emotions, to calm herself down, and to understand that this is nothing out of the ordinary. Mothering is a messy and interrupted experience. Her morning won't go to plan, as many others won't. She pulls herself together and realizes the most important thing is not to lose her cool—to stay fluid, to recalibrate. She helps Chevy choose new clothes and talks to Greg calmly about how to resurrect the project. The laundry won't be done, and she hopes maybe the Zoom call will, but if not, okay. She piles all the kids into the car and hopes they won't be late for school. On the way, she tells them a story from when she was a kid, and they all manage to laugh as they imagine their mom with pancake batter all over her jeans. Just as she drops them off, the bell rings, and she recognizes that she has done well...especially compared to last week's fiasco, when voices were raised. Something shifted for her this time. She understands that she has a choice in how to respond. If she is able to gather herself, to pause and think calmly, the situation is an opportunity to show her children, and herself, how to regulate during stressful times rather than catastrophizing. She's proud that this time she was able to control her impatience and panic and that she could even laugh with them instead of frowning and complaining. As she thinks about the encounter on her way home, she feels a little teary and overwhelmed by this small victory. She knows how many times she has messed up before and all too well how the alternative could have played out, hoping that next time or the one after, she will once more experience the same feelings of renewal and relief that are with her now. But who knows? Not so easy to do well every time, when life throws so many interruptions and curve balls across our paths.

While the generally accepted narrative is that as mothers we are interrupted by our children, it goes two ways: paradoxically, we also interrupt them. In her book, Baraitser shares her own experience of interruption. Her son Joel experienced some stammering after he received an accidental knock to his head when he was a toddler. Baraitser describes her concern about the stammer and her attempts to fix it, which included taking him to speech therapy. As the therapy unfolded, it became clear that a relationship existed between her son's stammer and her inability to bear the pain of this interruption to his speech. The speech therapist filmed the interactions and play between Baraitser, her partner, and Joel with subtle yet powerful results. Baraitser recounts what she saw in the replay of their session:

> There we are, always a step ahead, there, interrupting him...a gesture, a small movement of the hand towards the puzzle piece that he hasn't yet noticed, our fingers dexterously slotting the [pieces] together while he fumbles next to us, giving up, waiting instead to play with the tower we have made.[34]

Baraitser recognized that she was interfering with her child's play, and, rather than being reflective and patient with him, she was clearly unable to calm him or herself or to bear uncertainty. Her intrusion had spread to other areas of Joel's development, including his speech. In her eagerness to react quickly, to fix things that were bothering her, and to move on, she was actually contributing to rather than relieving his stammer. Discovering her own blind spot helped to resolve Joel's speech as much as the therapy did. Despite what Baraitser describes as a "drama of interruption,"[35] Joel's stammer disappeared over the next few months.

Mothering is a messy experience, but by making space for fluidity and focusing on being present, a mother can appreciate and bear the interruption despite the inner havoc that it creates for her. These everyday maternal interruptions have the potential to be so much more than a pesky nuisance, as they paradoxically fuel and renew the mother's experience if she is open to this.

The paradoxes of motherhood that I've pointed out so far culminate and meet with the most fundamental contradiction about mothering, this idea of maternal ambivalence. It is a vulnerable and chilling suggestion that a mother can possibly hold negative feelings together with her love toward her child. The baby books don't include a chapter on this subject, and the topic is taboo in online forums and on social media. The so-called funny memes are self-deprecating or condescending—such as mommy wine time, supposedly all that the mommy has the time or desire for after the kids are in bed. None acknowledge the true range of feelings that a mother experiences, and many in fact actively cover them up by encouraging her to laugh it off or show only her positive, perfect side to the world. That a mother can experience, much less talk about, these feelings of frustration, anger, and even flashes of hate toward her child goes against everything I have ever known about being a mother, but these feelings contain truth. This raises the question: How does she comprehend the possibility that these dark feelings are a key to renewing and fueling her love? Mothering is full of contradictions. We are on our way to coming to terms with the honesty that is maternal ambivalence.

THREE

THE ENOUGH MOTHER

IN BOTH MY PERSONAL AND professional life, I often ask myself two questions: What do most mothers strive for in their mothering? And how does a mother establish and recognize her own benchmarks for success? These queries aren't easy to respond to. A young mother I know articulates it best. Her forceful but heartfelt statement, "I just want to be enough," is both concise and meaningful, and guides my understanding; successful mothering is a feeling of what I refer to as *enoughness* for a mother. There are no descriptive words; it's just *enough*. While every mother has her own version of what is enough, equally, it's something recognizable. It's in that warm moment when a mother is in rhythm with her world and her child—a moment when it all makes sense. She is able to acknowledge and accept that she's doing the best job she can, given her limitations, of which there are many. Any moments of self-acceptance and self-forgiveness also help her to have compassion for her child. These are moments that replenish her and steel her for what's ahead.

We're all a work in progress, mothers being just as much so, if not more. From our missteps as mothers, we learn, repair, and recover, and eventually we understand that it's okay to be less than perfect; in fact, striving for perfection only raises the bar of motherhood to heights impossible to reach. And I believe that it is in these imperfect times that we have the opportunity to regain our equilibrium. To feel that we are enough. These are the moments where the universe briefly aligns and when our blunders actually make sense. We gain confidence that in spite of these lapses, we can keep moving forward and come to trust that moments like these will be recaptured many times. This hopeful state of mind isn't easy to reach or hold onto. One minute a mother grasps it, and the next it's gone. It is hard to preserve in the early, hands-on years of mothering, when every minute presents new possibility and there is so little time to think.

Enoughness is an active dynamic. It encourages us to be aware of and to challenge both our inner expectations and the external cultural ones. It urges us to be compassionate with our limitations and to check ourselves when we feel overwhelmed by fear, doubt, and impossibly high cultural standards. This poses questions of how we manage being flooded with uncertainty, not knowing what the future holds. T. H. Ogden[36] gives wise words to this daily and constant part of mothering. He reframes "not knowing"[37] as an opportunity to push forward despite the feelings of fear, confusion, and being lost that uncertainty brings to the mother. The mother who is enough can tolerate this turmoil. She can recover her equilibrium and get to her own truth despite the mess and confusion that everyday mothering brings. Her constant struggle to feel enough is buoyed by her ability to keep moving forward despite the fear of the unknown, her willingness to forgive herself and her child, and the power of the love she has for him.

I like the word "enough" because it fulfills certain conditions. It's a soothing word that limits expectations and judgment because it's so subjective; one person's understanding of enough will of course differ from another person's. This normalizes varying circumstances and allows for—even promotes—different levels of enoughness.

However, the idea of "enoughness" also raises questions in a mother's struggle to feel she is enough. What does "enough" or "good enough" really mean? How does a mother get to feel she is enough? How does she capture it? What does she let go of as she reconciles being enough? What does "enough" mean regarding her own identity? That of her children? Her partner? Her own mom? And wider society? How does she measure this and maintain it? Hold onto it and develop it?

My understanding of enough mothering is also drawn from the work of the British pediatrician and psychoanalyst Donald Winnicott, who devised the term "the good enough mother." He had a profoundly deep interest in the welfare of women and their babies, and he revolutionized a lot of the common thinking about motherhood. He kept the interest of mothers uppermost in his mind, writing books for them and for the general public in sincere, compassionate, and relatable language. His book *The Child, the Family, and the Outside World*[38] is dedicated to mothers having their first or second babies, who, he reminds his readers, are in a state of such primal dependency. Winnicott candidly described a mother's daily reality, full of challenges and efforts that often go unrecognized and unappreciated. His understanding of the centrality of a mother's well-being, both to her own and to her child's development, closely intersects with my work. His writing is clear and compassionate, addressed straight to mothers themselves, empathizing with their struggles and their joys, and capturing the essence of what a mother tries to be as she faces challenges and holds onto herself, both inside and out. Winnicott's soothing words urge the mother to listen and trust her own inner voice, as she is the one who knows her child best, and while he addresses the new mother, his sentiment is crucial for all stages of mothering.

Winnicott's work also courted controversy. His 1949 article "Hate in the Counter-Transference"[39] contains a section in which he discusses reasons why mothers might hate their babies. While his everyday examples might be considered a bit tongue-in-cheek and exaggerated, they hold truth. For example, he describes how a child treats his or her mother: "He is ruthless, treats her as scum, an unpaid servant, a slave," and "He is suspicious, refuses her good food, and makes her doubt herself, but eats well with his aunt."[40] As mothers, we can certainly identify. This was groundbreaking. While his language is a bit outdated, we get the message: we are allowed to have these feelings. While he placed, or some may say disguised, these words in an academic article, his message was clear and brave. For Winnicott, while everyday maternal reality can elicit feelings of hatred in a mother, he was challenging the mother to talk about and normalize her feelings. His words encouraged mothers to admit and accept their true feelings as being an inherent part of mothering. Facing her feelings of hatred rather than avoiding the unsavory parts of motherhood was a revolutionary idea, even for a thinker ahead of his time. He has made a massive contribution to this conversation.

Winnicott was also scathing of the idea of maternal perfection.[41] In his discussion of what he calls "infant-care," he rejects the place of perfection, insisting that perfection "belongs to machines" and that what the infant needs is "the care and attention of someone who is going on being herself."[42] This is the mother's humanity. While machines may be programmed—should be, that is—to ideal expectations and total perfection, the *enough* mother resists this. She frees herself enough of the time to be fluid, reliable, and present, and to enjoy her child. She reacts to interruptions or her child's behavior with measured patience instead of anger, frustration, or impulse enough of the time. Her enoughness allows her to accept her failures as part of mothering and as an opportunity to learn. It inspires her to realize that there will be future opportunities to mend her missteps or avoid them. These instances of repair allow her to find an inner space to restore her balance, to allow herself a sense of inner satisfaction, knowing that she is being the best mother she can be to her child at a given time, given her limitations, which she knows are many.

Edward Tronick, an American developmental psychologist, is best known for his work and research on the relationships between mother and infant. His book *The Power of Discord*[43] draws attention to the idea of attunement, "reaching for each other in sync, and in general matching each other's every move,"[44] and the value of mismatch and repair in all relationships. He cites research that supports the theory that attunement is in fact not the norm; rather, mismatch occurs 70 percent of the time in most relationships. While I consider that these statistics are quite startling, on further examination they allow us to shift the narrative that attunement is a given; rather, it becomes something to aspire toward, a goal. This is a reminder to us to be more open to the inevitable disharmonies that occur in our communications and to be creative and questioning of them. This idea echoes my work on mothering and the value I place on maintaining flow, despite the tension that emerges as the mother struggles with the mismatch and repair as she tries continually to realize attunement with her child. Sometimes she succeeds, and sometimes she fails, but she keeps moving forward.

The notion of time is a monumental test of a mother's feelings of her own enoughness. As new mothers, we are pressed for time, ruled by sleeping routines and eating schedules. We're at the mercy of time, whether in the seconds and minutes that tick by indefinitely or the years that suddenly disappear while we're preoccupied with everyday life. Motherhood is the most time-consuming job there is. Fitting our lives into a schedule heightens the daily tensions between the expectations that the mother places on herself and those that come from the outside world. Who does her time belong to? Is it hers to share with her child, or vice versa? The paradox is that the mother who isn't ruled by the minutes, who allows herself to run out of time as she relaxes, plays, and enjoys her child rather than continually watching the clock, is on an easier path toward achieving her enoughness. This is in contrast to a mother who feels that she isn't enough and is bound to struggle more with her discomfort as she attempts to do more and more in her precious time to compensate for her perceived failings. In their circular paths to achieve enoughness, it is clear that flowing with time surpasses being ruled by it. In fact, I ended my first book, *The Maternal Experience*,[45] with some musings and misgivings about my years of hands-on mothering titled "If Only I..." And I quote: "If only I had slowed down, been less serious and laughed more. Had I played longer at bath time, been willing for my children to be late to school a few times and insisted on less after school activities."[46] In hindsight, fluidity and presence trumps rigidity.

Enoughness shows us that there is power and resilience in repair, in the discomforts of mothering, in not being at the mercy of time but flowing with it as we learn to keep going despite the struggle that lies in not knowing where we are even going.

Trish was struggling. There was nothing in the world more meaningful to her than being a mom, and her son Adam had always been a total joy—a little boy brimming with curiosity and excitement, his active, bright mind open to discovery, full of innocent questions and play. However, when he turned four and started preschool, things changed dramatically. To Trish, it was as though the outside world had captured him, and she'd lost her little boy.

Trish was generally derailed by Adam's sudden change in behavior. "I was experiencing so many new and overwhelming feelings. His mood was different. When he came home from kindy, he just wanted to watch television. He was totally exhausted and of course irritable. One day as usual he climbed up on the kitchen stool so we could make a cake together, but I used the glass bowl instead of the metal one. He knocked it to the floor, smashing it. I told him not to worry, but he became so upset with himself that he was inconsolable. Another day, he had a friend over after school and wouldn't share his toys. Of course, there was a fight; Adam had a tantrum, which I didn't know how to handle other than giving him a time-out and calling the little boy's mom to come pick him up." Incidents like this were becoming more numerous, and as Trish puts it, "I was at the end of my tether. I felt like I was pushing a boulder up a steep hill most of the time, and the rock was close to crushing me. I felt like I was constantly failing as a mother, and that I couldn't fix things up like I used to. I just felt defeated and useless and that something in our lives was going awry. All I wanted was to be able to laugh and to enjoy him again."

Shortly after one of Adam's worst meltdowns, Trish suddenly remembered an email the school had sent out with the subject line: "A Mom's Guide to Starting Preschool." She hadn't opened it yet, treating it as a joke; no one knew her child better than she did. Now, in desperation, she decided to have a look.

It turned out that the school administrators and teachers, who had the benefit of seeing thousands of children and their parents experience the life-changing transition to school days, knew a thing or two about what to expect. The email candidly described the start of preschool as a double crisis for mother and child both. It described the circular relationship between a mother and child, and that while they impacted each other deeply, a mother would need above all to remain the adult while her child adjusted to being in a foreign place, meeting new people, and discovering a host of new ideas, routines, and social mores. It was now beginning to make sense to Trish, who realized she needed to be responsible for maintaining her calm, which is never an easy task. She needed to respond—that is, to first take the time to think—rather than to react to Adam's feelings, to distinguish them from her own in the moment. This called for her to be present and patient, to go at her child's pace, and to take her cues from him. By being curious, thoughtful, and caring, she was more likely to be flexible as opposed to rigid.

Flow helps to minimize expectations, what I call the *shoulds*, of mothering and to encourage laughter and humor. While starting preschool presents many unknowns for both child and mother, the email assured Trish that things would work out somehow, if not in the way that she'd foreseen. It was a reminder that everyday preschool life couldn't be perfect, but if it was enough, then she was doing well.

In the aftermath, Trish thought about how these words applied to her. We moms and our children really do affect each other deeply. She had to acknowledge the ways in which Adam had triggered her and how she'd responded. Was she being too serious in her reactions to his behavior? Laughter had always calmed both of them and reinforced their connection. "Who says the park is better than sitting down together watching television? In fact, Adam's teacher had told me he hadn't adjusted yet to napping at school, so no wonder he was coming home exhausted and cranky. Perhaps he wonders why he has to go to school at all and what I'm doing without him all day. When I remind myself that I'm doing the best that I can, and so is Adam, then I'm able to keep things in perspective and I feel better about myself. Aiming for perfection is not only useless, it's damaging, and it's much more reasonable to settle for being enough, which counters harshness and allows our love for each other to recharge itself." Sometimes, when the going gets rough, even moms need a time-out—a moment to step outside the drama of a situation, take a breath, and allow clarity to surface.

These words helped Trish to really comprehend the circular relationship that existed between herself and Adam. She recognized that she'd been short on concern and understanding and that she'd judged him too severely rather than putting herself into his shoes. Equally, she had been hard on herself and realized that she needed to be much kinder and more considerate all around. In other words, she needed to be the adult for both of them.

I keep returning to the word "enough," the idea that mothers need to see themselves as enough. When their loving feelings keep repairing themselves and stay in motion, then there is a sense within the mother that she is enough. Not perfect, not all-knowing—just enough.

This story also prompts me to think about Winnicott's good enough mother, and how the word "good" impacts a mother's daily experience. Does good contradict the flow of enough? Does it derail the mother who may doubt her goodness? Maybe it reminds her of the maternal ideal's rigid notions and expectations, which require her to be the ever-present and ever-caring mother, which she knows she isn't. She may feel insincere, that something is amiss: How can I be good if I make so many mistakes and I am not always as fully available and selfless as I should be? This sometimes puts even more pressure on her, raising fears about her own understanding of what "good" means and whether she is living up to that understanding. It may cause complications and unrealized expectations that she has about herself to be reignited. There is also the possibility that she'll feel deflated because she cannot identify or understand the idea in any way. Then there are issues about the impossibility of measuring goodness and the blurry notion of what good means.

So, I simply refer to the mother as enough. This avoids the shadow of judgment, invites fluid thinking, and reduces the problem of the maternal ideal. Flow, rather than rigidity, encourages the mother to think about how she sees herself, how society sees her, and how she can possibly manage this gap in between. The use of enough is more realistic and encourages a mother to create and live by her own definition of enoughness.

Ultimately, the enough mother surrenders to her own version of mothering. She acknowledges and opens herself up to the fullness of the experience by accepting all her feelings, which frees her to be okay with motherhood's messiness. She understands that all of her feelings need a voice and a place in her consciousness, even if some are too difficult to talk about. Her painful feelings and inner tensions have value. She shapes a thinking space to help her respond rather than react. A process of self-acceptance and compassion allows her to gather herself and mend her mistakes, trusting that next time or the time after she will do better. While her expectations about herself and outside social pressures continually threaten her balance, she can steady herself enough of the time. She normalizes her feelings. She discovers a rhythm that works for her enough of the time. She remains curious and bears the unknowns that she faces daily. Rather than ignoring her distressing feelings, she faces them head-on, despite her fear of and revulsion toward them. She becomes brave. There's movement and truth.

FOUR

THE LIE OF PERFECTION

DEEP INSIDE OURSELVES, EVERY MOTHER is convinced of certain realities that keep her going.

She is aware, even if the understanding is buried in her subconscious, that her mothering is full of many myths and taboos. They tempt her to be rigid when she needs to be fluid, and they tell her she needs to be totally selfless when in fact she can't ever really give herself away completely. Who isn't drawn into the lie of perfection?

Mothering is traditionally expressed in terms of extremes—that is, the mother is imagined as either all giving, tender, and devoted or its opposite: mean, selfish, and self-serving. Social media, arguably the most influential platform today for young mothers, generally mirrors this trend and divides mothering between something that is achievable in all its wonder and selflessness or an experience that is continually dismal. However, mothering is both, and while this truth is beginning to emerge, it isn't yet widely understood or accepted. The account of mothering that favors being moderate and inclusive, the *and* being important to note, is what I call *enough*, and it is my preferred narrative. It is distinct from those that encourage extremes and exclusivity, such as perfection *or* imperfection.

Typically, moms prefer to show happy, smiley, contented faces to the world. They prefer to send a message that all is good and that they are managing motherhood without a hitch. They convey positive feelings such as satisfaction, acceptance, gratification, patience, presence, and pride in their mothering. The catch is there's something untruthful here. It's not so wonderful all the time. So, what are mothers hiding when they only show this side, and more important, why are they hiding anything? As well as the joy and love, there is self-blame, guilt, shame, never-ending vigilance, worry, resentment, anxiety, hatred, and anger. Perhaps the most despairing feeling is the tedium, the absolute exhaustion that is a soul-destroying part of everyday life, which most mothers fear admitting to, even to themselves.

Emma, a stay-at-home mom, is the mother of an infant, a three-year-old, and a six-year-old. In another life, before having children, she was a banker, and in her own words: "The only things that I get to count now are socks. My life is so full of routine—cooking, cleaning, driving children to play groups, and grocery shopping. I feel like I'm on autopilot most of the time. It's almost impossible to find meaning in this tedium; some days make sense, others don't. I know that a big part of me wants to be at home, but I have traded part of myself away to that end. I used to be out in the world, a valued part of financial circles; I used to have something to say, and my colleagues would listen. Now I'm just a mother. But I know it's both. Sometimes I stare out of the window and think there must be more to life than this, and at other times I'm okay, especially when I get a hug or a smile from my child—the light shines bright for me then. So I would describe myself as somewhat satisfied. The funny thing is, despite climbing the walls, I'm not yet ready to take time out for myself. Go figure."

Why is sharing this reality still taboo—the daily grind, the exhaustion, the sheer ordinariness, and the struggle, along with the joys that make up daily life? There are still plenty of long-held maternal myths that affect mothers daily as we strive to distinguish between what looks perfect on the outside and what our inner reality contains, and the truth is that falling short often as a mother is what makes her human. It is also the only quality that allows her to grow— even to thrive.

It is in these moments of conflicting emotions that the enough mother has the presence of mind to use these feelings as a tool, almost as an engine rather than an enemy of her mothering. She notices that often her troubling feelings— moments such as those of irritation, exhaustion, resentment, and at times even pangs of hate—also renew and restore her love while attracting vital and softer emotions, including compassion, laughter, humor, hope, care, concern, gratitude, and pity. While she recognizes flashes of hate in her anger, she has come to realize that they are also present, although mostly in disguise, hiding under other more seemingly harmless emotions such as guilt, shame, and resentment. All these feelings offer ways to transform her hateful feelings into loving ones.

That young mother's raw plea, "I just want to be enough," continually echoes in my ears. There's a plain yet complicated truth in enoughness: it is a mother's battle cry to keep things real. The yearning, hoping, and praying to be enough is what guides us through daily life, both as mothers and as people. One of the primary aspects of this battle within, of course, is related to those two somewhat separate existences: mother and person. There is the combination of our internal disposition, our past and current life experiences, notably those with our own family of origin, what we saw as children, how we were mothered, and how we fit with our child. These memories and experiences are unconsciously, continually returned to throughout a mother's life in all of her interactions with her child.

There is a dance for the mother as she feels she is enough one minute, then not enough in the next, as she shifts between her inside and outside worlds. However, at times her inner world is dominated by a strong inner critic, who saps her self-confidence and seduces her by offering her a safe place to avoid the real pain of everyday mothering. This inner saboteur encourages the mother to play a role and to rely on an external ideal rather than the flow of her genuine emotions as a guide. This eats away at her feelings of enoughness and her own truth. By buying into this deception, her growth falters, and she becomes cut off from herself and her child. This can unsettle her and block her capacity for reflection and flow.

She also carries an unconscious fear that her destructive forces will destroy her love. This is usually met by a resurgence of deep loving feelings that I describe as melting moments, which almost wipe out her doubts and anxieties and recharge her love while pushing her on to keep going and struggling. It is a measure of her strength and her loving feelings that despite her inner conflicts, she maintains this dynamic. An enough mother has a moral barometer that helps to regulate her and her child and to maintain the idea that she is doing okay in her mothering enough of the time.

What can a mother do with these unspeakable feelings? If you've read this far, you're hopefully as convinced as I am that these emotions need their own space and cannot be disregarded or ignored. She realizes that they can teach her something. Can she see that the tension between her contradictory feelings, such as her pain, anxiety, worry, fears, and even flashes of hate, are a clue to something? Can she use them as a source of repair rather than shame or judgment? Is she open enough? The mother who is enough can give all her feelings a space and hold them together well enough as she hangs onto rather than disregards the gritty, uncomfortable, and taboo parts of herself.

There is a real danger in holding on too closely to taboo rather than embracing truth, especially in the early years of motherhood. We're usually younger, inexperienced, and riddled with doubts and concerns about whether we're doing the right thing for our children. Am I doing this the right way? Should I bottle-feed? Am I a bad mother if I don't like to breastfeed? And as a child gets older: When is the right time to send my child to day care? Can I go back to work? We worry and despair over one decision, until the next one pops up like a PEZ dispenser, and we lose confidence in ourselves entirely. Our fear of being labeled bad, unfit, selfish, lazy, and worse gets deeper and deeper unless we learn to normalize taboo. It can take a long time for the power that we give to taboo to diminish so it no longer controls us.

The enough mother develops and preserves an inner dialogue that reassures her that her struggles are normal despite the daily hardship and interruption. She cultivates and listens to her inner voice that assures her that she's okay, that she has a handle on her losses and missteps, and that she can manage her feelings of anxiety. She comes to terms with the dual reality of motherhood—the inseparable yet conflicted emotions it provokes—and learns that it is best for herself and her family to look at life anew through the lens of *and* rather than *or*. She surrenders to her contradictory feelings rather than silencing them. She owns the truth when she sits with the dissonant emotions of maternal ambivalence. While her distressing feelings overwhelm and shock her, in time she melts, which paves a way for surges of love and further enoughness. At the core of feeling enough, she maintains the belief that her loving feelings will always endure and have the power to absorb and overcome any moments of hate, which allows her to come to terms with her feelings of ambivalence. Even better, it allows her to aspire toward ambivalence rather than avoid it.

IDEALS AND EXPECTATIONS

There is a marked gap between every mother's hopes and dreams and the reality of what is, and as she navigates the tension between her inner and outer life, there is a clash between her expectations and her reality and the disquieting feelings that emerge in these spaces. I draw on two stories here, which demonstrate that despite the expectations that the maternal ideal prompts, the enough mother's flow can provide a buffer to her unsettling feelings.

Christa, the mom of a six-month-old baby named Tia, called me saying, "I'm feeling overwhelmed and anxious. I offered to look after my friend's baby for a few hours, and now I realize it's just too much for me. Tia needs my full attention, and I need to be there for her. What happens if they both start crying at the same time? I'd be torn. I want to tell Patty that I can't help her out this time, but what will she think of me? I'm scared of letting her down and that it will affect our relationship. I don't know why I can't cope with something so basic; some people have three children under the age of four, and I just have one. But I feel this so strongly. Mothering is the hardest thing I have ever done—so many feelings that are fighting each other all the time that I need to consider." This new mother struggled with her decision but knew that the welfare of her own baby, her friend's baby, and her own well-being weighed most heavily. The deep pull of her genuine feelings allowed her to be aware of her limits and to reject the pull of social expectations as she was able to process and think about her options. Her inner strength and knowing won as she gathered the courage to say, "I can't," to herself and her friend and to the expectation that she could do it all. By speaking up, she demonstrated that she is enough of a mother. It's inspiring and brave, and guess what? In the end, she told her friend about her concerns, who understood fully.

This story is a reminder of the daily maternal challenges. There is a gap between her expectations of herself, what she assumes a mother can achieve, and what her own reality is. The enough mother spends a lot of her day reconciling her own ideals with those belonging to others as she struggles to keep in check the parts of her that want to be able to do it all, to be perfect. She has an awareness on some level that perfection stifles her humanity and is not possible, but it is so difficult not to aim high. And it is so hard not to feel as though she's giving up too easily. But she listens to all of her feelings and is honest with herself about them. Rather than dismissing the uncomfortable ones, she flows with them and accepts them and somehow muddles through her day. She owns her feelings of ambivalence. Mothering is simply—and complicatedly—a kaleidoscope of emotions.

A year later, as Christa held her new baby twins, she could see the irony in her previous challenge as a first-time mom. "Now I know that babies have an inner homing device that makes them cry in unison! Today I have my own orchestra of screaming babies, and looking after two for just a couple of hours would be a breeze. I have a completely different perspective now, and a sense of flow and a sense of humor are my new best friends."

Another new mother, Andy, struggled with insecurity when she measured herself against her friend Bea. Bea was up early every day, her daughter neatly dressed and ready to go to the park at 9 a.m. to meet friends. She had the housework under control, left no mountains of laundry behind her, and managed to cook dinner for her husband every night. She even entertained friends on the weekends. What a dynamo. Andy couldn't conceive of how this was possible. She loved being at home, only venturing out on daily errands when necessary, and her husband had taken over meal preparations. In her own words: "I feel so inadequate."

I tried to reassure her that every mother is different and that she had to run her own race and not worry about others. All of my advice seemed useless until I sent her an article about new moms.[47] "Margo, that part about how all new moms rely on some sort of coping mechanism made it so clear for me. Now I get it. Bea copes by organizing, going out, seeing people, being busy, whereas I manage by going slowly, spending time alone with Cara. We just have found our own ways to survive new motherhood. Her way isn't better than mine—it's just different. It's not helpful for me to judge myself. Everyone relies on some sort of coping mechanism, not just me."

This is Andy's earned wisdom. She removed herself from the internal race with Bea, which represented false expectations and what she felt that she ought to be doing, and instead worked on normalizing and valuing her own experience rather than judging it. Andy's light-bulb moment allowed her to open herself up to another way of thinking and feeling, and while her inner policeman had lost part of her job, she was still hanging around, waiting for an opportunity to pounce. Andy's experience is a warning to moms that the inner critic who demands perfection will never be satisfied, whereas the willingness to be a little gentler on ourselves and to own our enoughness will help us to remain more engaged and confident in our mothering.

I ask the question: How does a mother hold onto her loving feelings through all this? The day-to-day pressures and disruptions are often enough to destabilize any mother as she fights to hold onto her belief that she's enough of a mother, even though (and because) she lost her temper three times today or she forgot to respond to an email from the preschool teacher. She is tormented by the will-this-ever-end doubts, together with the exhaustion, boredom, and tedium of her mothering. Add to this extra stress factors, including finances, work, family difficulties, and extraordinary situations, such as illness or COVID.

A mother's feelings and actions are colored by internal feelings, by the hazy, confusing and ever-changing lines that characterize the relationship with her child. Her child is so much a part of her that they share a unique emotional and physical bond, but they are still separate. How does the mother navigate the paradox and complications that this brings? She often feels torn. She most likely both dislikes and enjoys the time and energy that she puts into her child and the reliance they have on each other. She may feel simultaneously satisfied and suffocated, and probably hates herself for feeling the latter. When she is away from her child, she may feel a yearning to be with him, and when she's at home, she's climbing the walls. She has moments when she desperately wishes to be somewhere else, but often she can't share this feeling with anyone. She feels guilty about wanting to have her own space, but she longs for it. In the early years, an uninterrupted shower would do marvels. She is often caught between who she needs to forgive. Is it herself for her actions and feelings, or her child for not living up to her imaginings? It's a very complicated dynamic for anyone to live with.

Maternal feelings of love are complicated and are "almost always found in combination with other emotions such as possessiveness, jealousy, resentment, tenderness, pride, loyalty, longing, admiration, desire,"[48] says Hester Solomon. These are the words of a mother I interviewed: "I love my child, but some days I just can't stand mothering—the everyday stuff, the routine, the boredom, the guilt, the shame, and the worry. That's just a few of my daily emotions. In saying this, my child is my life. There's fun, there's laughter, there's gratitude, there's tears of joy and pain. The person who coined the term "groundhog day" got it right. It describes a mother's life, especially in the first few years. When they get older, it's different; it's still intense and challenging but in a new and often more complicated way."

These lines shine a light on two universal truths of motherhood. The first is that all of our feelings are transient, except for the love we always have for our children. The second is that the time we are committed to spending with them is finite. Eventually, this part of our job will end. Acknowledging our emotions allows us to be more fully present during these precious years, for both our children and ourselves, and to receive the gifts of motherhood more completely.

RESENTMENT

Then there are the feelings of resentment, which most mothers experience at some point (or more often) during their mothering. These feelings of displeasure or indignation or anger are all part of being a mother. Some mothers are more willing to claim these feelings than others: the mother who can admit that she is "fed up" with her mothering and who can't stand it anymore; the mother who says things like, "I'm pulling my hair out," or, "I can't fricking stand this anymore," or, "I'm at the end of my tether." Her words are expressed in everyday language and are sometimes softened with a bit of humor, but by owning her feelings, she frees herself to keep going with her mothering; she gets herself out of a rut. She's revealing some of the truth that moms don't usually admit to but that they live with every day. By challenging the ideal out loud, something that is usually forbidden, we see her humanity; she's not hiding her feelings. Perhaps there is even something deeper lurking here—the honesty that she both deeply loves her child more than anything, but at times, moments, seconds, she also fricking hates all this, her child, her life, and herself. By admitting this, she feels better. She's renewed. She is expressing her maternal ambivalence. And if she has some friends who can share and chant their mom truths together, then all the better. Our confessions often revive us.

We're entitled to our feelings of resentment and annoyance during the days that consist of continual demands on our bodies and minds, along with the fairly consistent absence of appreciation or thanks, as much as we resent their very existence too. Of course, our own childhood experiences affect how we mother, and there are plenty of emotions stirred up unpredictably. When we can locate these feelings and air them positively, particularly when we align them with practical expectations, we have the best chance to regulate our responses and to get happier outcomes.

Katie, whose daughter Gia is now fifteen, looks back on those early days of mothering. "I was exhausted, and I often had a lump in my throat. I didn't know where to put myself much of the time. It started with being up most nights for hours with Gia screaming with teething pain. Her screams exhausted, frightened, and frustrated me. That feeling of not being able to comfort her. Then, to add insult to injury after I spent all this time cooking special meals for her, she refused to eat anything but store-bought yogurt. I remember from the time she turned four, when she could tell me what she wanted, we found a way to talk to each other, despite a few roadblocks. Now she's fifteen, and I'm often still struggling with that same lump in my throat."

Katie reflects often on how her past impacts her everyday experience. "I know it's partly because I come from a big family, and as the oldest daughter, I shouldered a lot of the responsibility for my siblings. I married young, and now I feel the weight of so many years of duty, which is probably partly why we decided to stop growing our family at one child. It doesn't feel like I had much of a childhood. Sometimes I can feel the resentment oozing out of me. I'm yearning for something else, some freedom maybe, but I'm not sure. I'm so confused. On one hand, I often resent the way she treats me, but I can't voice this easily, so of course I send her mixed messages. I don't ask Gia to do much around the house, probably because I was expected to do everything when I was young, so I wanted to break that cycle. But when she doesn't even say thank you or offer to help a little, I get resentful. The other night, I stayed up till ten p.m. to cook her dinner after her dance practice. No thank-you, no nothing. She ate dinner while FaceTiming with friends. I felt so unappreciated and unseen.

"Last night I couldn't hold my feelings in anymore, so I told her how I felt. I became very emotional, and for once I didn't protect her from my truths. I felt overwhelming relief at being able to be so open. I now know when I feel resentful, I have to put words to this; it helps me, and it helps her. I need to show her that I'm brave enough to speak my mind even when there is the possibility of conflict. The other side to all this has been my ability to stay connected with her despite our issues. I'm the mom, and I need to make that happen. At the end of every day, no matter how displeased I am, I know I can give her a hug. I'm so grateful to be able to do that, and I'm also amazed that she has never tried to push me away. In our hugs, there are no words, just a lot of feeling, and then tensions subside. I need to take the lead and yet be soft; there's no room for pride or control. In a word, there needs to be flow. It's funny, I think I let go of my resentment in two opposing ways, by talking and not talking. When I voiced my feelings in words and told Gia how I felt, there was relief. By not talking and just hugging, we keep our relationship on track and alive. By holding her, and myself, physically and emotionally, at the end of the day, I think we are saying that it's okay to have difference. We still love each other, and there is still lots of work to do. We can be in sync despite having tense words. I make sure we don't shut down on each other—to be precise, that I don't allow my resentment to shut me down."

While this exchange had a positive outcome, I need to add a warning here. Katie had the capacity to process her feelings, to remain an adult, and to emotionally hold herself and her daughter while she spoke her mind without judgments or accusations. This is very different from a mother carelessly dumping her feelings onto her child without reflection or consideration. Taking into account the age of any child and one's ability to deliver a message calmly needs to be considered before a discussion like this proceeds.

With this in mind, though, this story shows how difficult feelings can actually be transformed into positive ones that strengthen a relationship. The common ground here is that although these mothers are dissatisfied, something motivates them to push through to higher ground. Their love remains.

GUILT AND SHAME

Guilt and shame feature prominently in nearly every mother's life. They are similar yet distinct emotions, and how they differ from each other offers an insight into the unsettling feelings that make up so much of mothering. Maternal guilt is connected with the feeling that an action is wrong, whereas maternal shame goes much deeper: it's a mother's sense that there's something wrong with her. A mother's feelings of guilt and shame, which she often experiences as sorrow or self-recrimination for hurting her child in some way, are at first somewhat indistinguishable from each other. Both are a result of the tension between a mother's inner experience and the pressures that she feels from the outer world. As time passes, and she develops patience and forgiveness toward herself, a mother's response to her pain unfolds in different ways. The mother who experiences guilt is usually able to confine her feelings to a particular occurrence that doesn't reflect her best intentions and is able to let go of some of her pain and begin to heal. While her heartache still lingers, she is able to separate from it most of the time, knowing that the opportunity to react differently in a similar situation will arise. This is the experience of the enough mother, who can harness her fluidity and her openness, who can repair her outlook for the future. Her image of herself remains whole. In saying that, an enough mother might contain her guilt for years. When it is again triggered, her original feelings may come flowing back, and for a few moments, she may be transported back to the incident. However, her guilt doesn't paralyze her. Guilt is fluid, the enough mother is aware, and she can stand to re-experience her feelings without being stranded or defined by them; she is able to bear and grow from them.

New mother of two, Jinny, is feeding her newborn son so peacefully that she is lulled almost into a trance herself. Suddenly, her three-year-old daughter, Tess, interrupts her by pulling at her sleeve and asking her to play a game. The mother raises her voice and angrily retorts, "Can't you see I'm feeding the baby now?" The toddler runs out of the room crying. Jinny is plagued by guilt. "Why did I lose my temper? She is also little and needs me." Jinny finishes the feed and apologizes to Tess, who is playing with dolls and seems to have forgotten the incident. However, Jinny cannot forgive herself. She keeps replaying the scene in her mind, which intensifies her guilt. At this point, luckily, Jinny makes a determined decision to rethink and to be curious about what happened. She realizes that she has a choice to make: "I can either learn from my experience and try to do better next time, or I can stay paralyzed in my guilt. I choose to learn." By doing this, Jinny is opting for a creative, empowering way to deal with her guilt and to move forward. She reflects on how to manage this situation when it occurs next time, knowing that she needs to find another way, determined next time not to raise her voice or become impatient. "Perhaps we can feed our babies together. Tess can feed her doll while I feed the baby." An awareness of her feelings together with a sense of flow allows Jinny to struggle, to feel regret, to mend her mistake, and to find a way to relieve her guilt. By being mindful of her feelings, she can develop what I call a patience space, which prompts the mother to stop and consider her situation before she responds—that is, to reflect rather than react. This includes reconciling her own expectations and needs with those of her little girl enough of the time. This interaction demonstrates what I call transformative guilt, which allows the enough mother to acknowledge her mistake to herself and her daughter and then to move forward. She can process and hold her regrets and disappointments at what she has done while she pardons herself.

The fluid nature of Jinny's guilt marks it from the experience of shame. Shame is inflexible and severe and doesn't offer much room for repair or relief. Rather than self-forgiveness and acceptance, shame tends to linger—whether for days, weeks, or decades, it deeply affects how a mother feels about herself. A mother who is mired in feeling ashamed of herself is unable to differentiate between her regrettable actions or mistake and her very being. If her reaction to her child was bad, then she must be a bad mother. She identifies so strongly with any one event or situation that she is unable to create a boundary between the two. They are one and the same in her mind.

My colleague Barbara's mothering was often deeply colored by shameful feelings and encounters. She had an internal critic who relentlessly judged her as a bad or good person and mother. It was a torturous, exhausting way to live, tracing far back to her early experiences of being judged by her own mother, who herself lived by the strict moral and religious codes handed down to her through her own mother. The mother-child dynamic had been transmitted through the generations. If Barbara left Cindy with a dirty diaper too long, she was a bad mother. If Cindy finished her lunch, Barbara was a good mother. Barbara's inner scorekeeping continued all day long. There was no escape. If Cindy was out in the sun without a hat and got a little sun, Barbara went straight to her default position: "I am a bad mother." There was no possibility for reflection and simply acknowledging, "I made a mistake that I feel guilty about. We all fail and that's okay. Next time, I'll bring sunscreen and a hat for her." Barbara's sense of self was totally defined by her actions. She was trapped in this cycle of shame—and perfection. There was no fluidity or mindful presence—only rules and automatic default switches. Her actions fell into strict categories of black or white. There was no gray area, no self-forgiveness—only rigidity. Without acknowledging this and developing the ability to process these emotions and move forward differently, she was setting Cindy up to live the same way too.

One day, it finally became too much for Barbara. She had been reading a book about mothering, and a few things struck her. She had never thought about how mothering styles pass through the generations and how important flow is; she'd always thought keeping to the rules was the only way to mother. She had answered a quiz in the book, and she scored very high on being a rigid mother. Suddenly, it all made sense to her. "I needed to step up and mother Cindy in my own way. I was emotionally and physically drained trying to live up to this fixed style of mothering, which is built on shame and guilt. It was obvious to me that I was mothering in exactly the same way I was mothered, without thinking about it. But it wasn't my mom's fault; this was on me. No one else was to blame. I needed to loosen up and somehow become aware of the fears and tension I am carrying, so that even a few more laughs wouldn't go astray."

Then came the daily test, and this time she passed. Barbara was pushing Cindy on the swing when her mom started in on her: "You are pushing her too high; she will fall; she will hurt herself." Instead of the usual torrents of self-blame and anxiety, Barbara pulled herself together, and the next few words just came out of her mouth, calm and in charge: "Mom, I love you, but I need to change how I mother. You have been a great mother to me, but now it's my turn to look after Cindy; she is my responsibility. You are her grandmother, and it's your job to have fun with her, not to bring her up. I need to do that my own way. It won't be perfect; I'll certainly make mistakes, but that's how I will learn. I'll recover from them and keep going. I won't get trapped in them. I'm human, not a robot. I will learn to forgive myself and keep moving forward. I need to flow in my mothering and enjoy her; that's my priority." It was the first of many steps in Barbara's transformation.

Experiences of guilt and shame loom large in a mother's life. They are alike to the extent that they can overwhelm anyone, and they are often mired in fear and uncertainty. The way that they surface depends on how a mother chooses to manage her concerns and the unknown. The mother who can hold onto her flow, who can step away from her emotions and observe them, is able to continue with a sense of hope for the future, a reassurance that all will generally be okay. She is able to take a break from her troubling feelings for long enough at least to break the cycle and to allow the possibility of her enoughness to prevail. She can admit, "I did that, I'm sorry for it, and now my job is to accept responsibility for the harm that I did and to move on and forgive myself." While acknowledging guilt is a challenge, it has healing properties too, whereas shame is a purely unsympathetic force. Guilt is the shadow from which we can step out into the sunlight; shame colors everything in the same shades of hopelessness. Barbara's initial internal conversation was riddled with doubt and negative thoughts about herself. She compared herself to others—and to an impossible maternal ideal—and fell short each time. Her confidence was shot; she was never enough, until one day when she figured it out. Her rigidity and attempts to be perfect and to avoid failures were blocking her creativity, her flow, and her self-expression—all signs of a mother's humanity.

ANGER

One of the most unacceptable, silenced, and common aspects of mothering is anger. Barbara Almond describes maternal aggression as "one of those societal problems that fills us with outrage and horror, even as some part of us secretly understands its normality."[49] This exposes the dilemma that exists at the heart of maternal fury: it is shocking and yet reasonable. In fact, COVID brought this oft-hidden dynamic into the public eye perhaps more so than any scholar or research has in the past. Reams of newsprint, millions of memes, and polls and studies on the division of household responsibilities have revealed the extreme pressures mothers face daily, extraordinary circumstances or not.

But how to talk about this taboo area? Is there any possibility that rage has redeeming features? As disturbing as this conversation is, it is vital to an understanding of the stigma surrounding anger in mothering. When a mother is unnerved enough to lose her temper, she must face the reality that her reaction isn't okay but that she is human and will make mistakes. A mother's explosion of feelings, especially her aggressive outbursts, usually provokes a cycle of self-recrimination, guilt, and shame. It also invariably attracts a lot of social judgment, whether real or perceived, as any mother who has lost it with a misbehaving child in public can attest.

Joyce Edward writes that most mothers experience deep regret when recalling the times that "they lost it"[50] with their children. Edward recounts the graphic recollections of a mother who "found herself after a sixth unsuccessful attempt to quiet her, starting to shake the baby."[51] The woman, who is now a grandmother, is still haunted by this memory of an event from forty-five years ago.

Jacqueline Rose, author of *Mothers: An Essay on Love and Cruelty*,[52] nails it. She exposes a primal contradiction, one of the deepest enigmas of mothering. That, for a mother, "there is nobody in the world I love as much as my child, nobody in the world who makes me as angry."[53] Rose's words are naming ambivalence, when a mother is faced with profound conflicting yet true emotions and the idea that our children, who inspire our deepest love, are also our most stinging triggers. A mother's angry outburst, like anyone else's, is often in part a reaction to past feelings and experiences. She might be transported back to her own childhood—circumstances when she felt helpless, dependent, and powerless, reviving a host of unresolved feelings of anger. When we expect our child to behave in a certain way and it doesn't happen, our first reaction is disappointment. Rather than thinking, finding that patience space, we resort to blame, an impulsive reaction. An angry maternal outburst follows, then feelings such as sorrow or regret.

Reacting immediately to psychological triggers is a trap many of us learn to recognize. Our triggers throw the balance of power within each of us into disarray, even briefly, knocking us out of the present and away from our sense of self. A mother is in the best place to correct this imbalance when she recognizes and accepts that she must rely on and be responsible for her own feelings, needs, and expectations. These belong to her, not her child. By taking charge of her disappointment and acknowledging her triggered feelings, she is fostering healthy separation, both within herself and between herself and her child. Jinny initially directed anger and blame at her toddler before realizing that her expectation for an uninterrupted feed needed examination, not her toddler's behavior.

Rage also builds up and has a tendency to erupt unexpectedly because there isn't a place for it to safely sit and be heard. But just as monitoring cholesterol and blood pressure every so often is important, as well as screening for cancer, early detection can make all the difference. While expressed maternal rage is overt and identifiable, a mother's passive rage remains less easy to diagnose or treat. It is often viewed by women and society as a more acceptable option, but it is equally, if not more, destructive in the long run. Its symptoms may include incidents of withdrawal, deafening silence, expressions or gestures of disapproval, or verbal put-downs, and while it may seem to "just be" a stern tone of voice, these forms of anger can be more protracted and menacing, affecting a child as deeply as more explicit forms of anger and rage.

Our maternal actions have reactions, and our maternal reactions do, too. Motherhood, as author and performer Minna Dubin has written, "is a relentless provocation!"[54] Dubin's article on mom-rage in the *New York Times* also contains an unforgettable comeback: "As if rage has never shared a border with love."[55] This is a remarkably fitting segue into the discussion of maternal ambivalence, rooted in taboo feelings that exist in all of us and also fuel our love.

LET'S NOT CIRCLE AROUND THE TRUTH.

Teri, a mother, confesses: "Some days I'm just fed up with my life. Don't get me wrong, I love my child, but each day is a slog. So much of it is routine. The chores are never-ending, and no one appreciates my doing them anyway. The walls feel like they're closing in, moments of enjoyment and fulfillment weighed down by the other stuff. I feel like I'm stuck between these parts of me. But there's something else happening here too. While it's okay, even socially acceptable, to hate the things that you have to do as a mother, or to admit to my own self-hatred—like I hate myself for not wanting to do what's expected of me—whoa, I can't hate being a mother.

"But does this cut it for me? I feel like I'm circling around the truth. I want just once to freely say, 'I love my daughter to the moon and back, but I have moments when I damn well hate mothering.' It might allow me to get back to being the enough mother. It makes me feel better to say it, and it makes my love more real. It's my truth and my words. I know my friends aren't comfortable with saying it, or even hearing it, and I wonder about that. Am I a shocking mother, or are they dishonest? Most likely both. I also know that by dancing around this, by avoiding this word, I'm missing out on an authentic part of my mothering. Voicing this lets me get on with it. I'm also so aware of the danger of cutting off, not caring, feeling indifferent. There's no coming back from that if my elastic limit is broken. If I'm stretched so thin that I can't get back to my love, that's not a place I want to be in—I'm sure of that. I know that I'm not the only one who feels like that, and maybe I can help other mothers to be more truthful and let them give all these taboo feelings a place. In a way, saying this clears and renews me. And now all the other feelings can come out, and we manage to keep breathing and to keep living. It doesn't kill us. It never ceases to astound me how my love for her works and keeps growing. My love as a mother always wins, but it's hard."

Teri's words are powerful, disturbing, and shocking, but eerily sound. She knows that these flashes of hate also carry intense love. The relationship between love and hate, while silenced and dirty, is a tolerated aspect of most intimate relationships. When it comes to mothering, the taboo sets in with rigor and intolerance. Despite its messiness and distasteful nature, the truth is that all close relationships hold love and hate to differing degrees. When tested, the strength of love can provoke hatred. Inactive love dulls the feeling and immobilizes most other emotions. David Mann, in his article "In Search of Love and Hate," writes that while love and hate are in opposition, they actually "passionately bind the subject to the object,"[56] meaning that mother and child are fused together by these oppositional feelings. In "Introduction: The desire for love and hate (By way of a poetic polemic),"[57] he writes that "the pendulum of love and hate never seems to stop. Perhaps love and hate are the only true perpetual motion."[58] A mother's capacity to be fluid is so integral to her ability to manage these feelings. Her flashes of hate occur in the context of flow, which allows her to say it and then move on, returning her to her child with a stronger sense of love.

Hazel, the mother of an eleven-month-old baby, recounted a most interesting moment that occurred in a mothers' group. One of the moms, Rebecca, suddenly said, "Sometimes I just can't stand being a mom." There was an extremely awkward pause, and then another mother chipped in, "So annoying, the teething!" as a way to break the tension, completely glossing over what Rebecca had said. Hazel pulled her aside when everyone resumed talking and explained that she totally understood. Her story made me wonder anew why it's so hard for women to express the negative emotions that come hand in hand with motherhood. Just because you are frustrated, it does not mean you don't love your baby. Just because you have moments of wanting to prioritize yourself, it doesn't make you any less of a mother. It makes you human.

Let's not forget the impact of social media. It usually shows one side or the other, whereas the truth is that everyday mothering is both, and from one minute to the next it changes. These days, social media is an influential part of our lives, especially in the case of young mothers, where it is often the first port of call for information and advice. It is always accessible, and it can be a relentless noise, particularly for young moms. It can be confusing, as it can make mothers feel both alone and not alone—we've become accustomed to the internet voices so much so that we feel we know them and that they are speaking directly to us. The abundance of discussion platforms in social media becomes a core part of mother's borrowed and learned experience, and it is her responsibility to be alert to what is useful, what is pointless, and what may be harmful. While much of it can be helpful, it is important to be aware of its drawbacks and to be critical and questioning when interacting with it. For example, when participating in an ongoing conversation, it is important to be mindful about being drawn into uncomfortable exchanges and to always be cautious about the content—

don't believe everything you see and read. On social media posts, such as Instagram and Facebook, just as in old-fashioned face-to-face groups, realize that these moms have an angle, so try to work out what it is. Dispose of superficialities and ideals that are heavily relied on in social media. Be honest about your own particular mothering experience; own it and release your inner critic. Use humor but don't laugh off your pain; it's telling you something. Let's show our struggles earnestly and try to learn from them. Let's be compassionate for the mother who is drowning in her despair. Let's honor both the ordinary victories and failures in every mother's day.

I learn from the mother who pays attention to her signals and doesn't avoid them, no matter how uncomfortable and distressing they are. The mother who is brave enough to own her feelings of anger, resentment, shame, and guilt, even as the maternal ideal tries to stymie them. She understands the danger of indifference, the experience of cutting herself off from her inner self and her child. I learn from the mother whose enoughness allows her to give the best she can while she struggles with her worries and anxieties and then applauds herself for this. I learn from the mother who wants to know her different parts, those that nurture her and the others that disrupt and make her feel uncomfortable and inadequate. I learn from the mother who battles daily to maintain her sense of flow and who must continually adapt to and struggle against long-held maternal myths and taboos, whether her own or those of others. I learn from the mother who really knows and engages with her true feelings, who listens to them, and who lets them speak to her. I learn from the mother who is courageous enough to know that while she often feels inadequate, her humanity and truth is what is important. It's the only way we get through this. Motherhood, that is.

FIVE

LET'S TOUCH TABOO

TABOOS ARE MAINTAINED THROUGH THE maternal ideal—the concept that there is one acceptable way to parent correctly, one way to be the right mother, one way to raise and love a child. The maternal ideal is the cultural fabric in which a woman mothers. We are deeply affected both by our personal experiences of being mothered and our social context. The ideal and its expectations are defined for us and by us, and our beliefs in those definitions become entrenched. In the early years of mothering, especially, the ideal holds a dominant place as both a guide and a burden. And, it paradoxically guides and misguides. It provides rules and limits that help to support a mother in her daily life, including the times when she is feeling fragile, when she feels that she has lost her way. These guidelines are socially acceptable and yet so rigid. They can provoke feelings of shame, guilt, and doubt as she tries to fulfill both her own and society's unachievable expectations. While any mother can become paralyzed by these demands, they also offer an opportunity for fluidity as she elects to struggle against these prescriptions and to learn to mother in her own way. While the maternal ideal represents the mother as selfless and ever present, which in theory are qualities to strive for, it still puts unrealistic pressure on her in an uncanny and surprising way by giving her the hope that she can be this ideal mother. It was pointed out to me by a young woman who was at a stage of intense mothering with two young children under the age of four, during the peak of COVID, that while she knew that negative feelings existed, bringing them to the fore and articulating and normalizing them actually made her feel less of a mother. Maybe there was a fear that contemplating these feelings might compromise and contaminate her love. Such is the complexity and the diversity of mothering.

I'm curious about how these jumbled and despairing taboo areas obstruct maternal well-being. The myth of maternal perfection is a glaring illustration. While I mentioned before that perfection is unattainable, Winnicott really hammers home the point by insisting, "it belongs to machines not mothers."[59] We continue to sabotage ourselves by believing that we can attain it, by imagining that it is possible and even worthwhile. It is exacting and hard to dismantle this myth because it goes right to a mother's long-held illusions about herself. By delving into the reality of the mother's daily life with compassion and curiosity, rather than judgment and expectations, we can realize an opportunity to challenge both our own and society's existing ideals about mothering and the taboos that hold them so high.

What is so useful about the maternal ideal? What does it contribute to our happiness as mothers, to the happiness and well-being of our families, and why as a society do we tend to hold onto it so firmly?

In this chapter, I'm going to turn the ideal upside down and ponder moments when a mother becomes really unhinged, that maternal underbelly (no pun intended) when the going really gets tough, and what we can learn from the moments, minutes, or hours when we're brought to our knees. I'm going to explore what it takes to push through these incredible barriers, what doing so exposes about a mother's raw self, and what keeps her going.

Whether you're the mom who's lost it in front of children and spouse, screamed your frustration and stormed out of the house for a few hours, or the one who tamps it down inside, howling instead into the metaphorical (or literal) pillow in quiet, we all reach the end of our tether eventually—and, most of us would admit, repeatedly.

These are the uncomfortable feelings and agonizing outbursts that we don't like to admit to or think back on, even to ourselves. The moments we try to dismiss and silence. The ones that we sweep under the carpet but that somehow escape and resurface, usually when we least expect them to. And they shock and surprise us every time, and even worse, they keep happening because these feelings are an undeniable part of our everyday life. It's clear that we cannot escape them, so I'm curious about what happens when we take the reverse path—if, instead of rejecting them, we lean into them and learn from them. What if we turned them upside down and reframed them as valuable feelings? I'm interested in what we can learn by exploiting the taboo around motherhood. By engaging with and trying to understand these experiences, can we open our minds to a more empowered, genuine, and meaningful mothering? This chapter is about what happens when we are so bound to our ideals, and to holding certain taboos in place to support our version of what we believe mothering should be, that we lose our way.

The recent dominance of television series in the media over the past decade has become more than just entertainment. It has given us the opportunity to immerse ourselves in the lives of others from the safety and distance of our own homes. I'm thinking in particular of those series that feature predominantly female characters who are famous for their own personal lives and career success. They've become a powerful medium for aspiration and fantasy but also for self-reflection and examination. One such actress is Reese Witherspoon, whose character, Elena, in the series *Little Fires Everywhere*[60] is an inspired example of the walking contradictions of motherhood. She presents a layered depiction of mothering and all its complications—and a lesson about what can happen when we keep the uncomfortable, messy parts of our life hidden and separate from the acceptable veneer we build up, when we think we can live our lives dodging reality, cloaked in taboo, and always reaching for the ideal. While Elena's story is not all of ours, it speaks to the conflicted humanity in all of us. I, for one, cannot help but recognize myself in her experiences on some level, even if I don't always want to admit it. Given the popularity of the series, I can only imagine many other women do too. Elena's experiences surprise and shock our sense of what's appropriate and acceptable, but in doing so, they expose issues that are at the heart of mothering for all of us.

Elena's home life is very much a snapshot of the upper middle class in American suburbia. She's well educated; married to a successful lawyer; and has four teenage children, a part-time job as a journalist, and a large, beautifully maintained home—the American Dream. Her children are well dressed, and there is a heavy importance placed on the right schools, as well as sports and music. There are family dinners with heated discussions and a family room where the children gather to watch television, eat snacks, and squabble. As the head of house, Elena runs everything like clockwork, with a near-obsession for doing things the "right," socially acceptable way.

She tightly schedules and supervises her household. A color-coded wall calendar occupies a place of prominence in the kitchen, with the children's activities charted in detail, which matches the perfectly color-coded lunch bags that Elena hands to each child as she sends them off to school each day. She drives her children to their extracurricular activities, attends school band nights, and is relentless about the importance of her children getting into the "right" colleges, that first step on the path toward their own perfect adult lives.

However, we wonder who she is doing the "right" things for: Is it for her family or herself? We soon realize that what Elena is willing to show to the world is not the whole story, and cracks appear in her perfectly presented life. Her polished exterior is just that—a façade. She is a study in contradiction. While she laughs and seems light and friendly at first, we soon see that she is truly rigid in many ways. She talks but she doesn't listen. Her curiosity seems to be self-serving. She has limited self-awareness. She's a journalist who ironically forces her children to comply with what they're told rather than to question or investigate.

While these family dynamics are not unusual, they shine a light on how we manage our own mothering—the role of judgment and expectation and the legitimacy of the maternal ideal. The superficiality of Elena's life is exposed on many levels. She deludes herself into thinking she is a pillar of the community. She leads a campaign, steered by her belief in her own moral high ground, about who the rightful mother is in an adoption dispute. Ironically, while she is busy on this crusade, she is totally unaware of the strife and division in her own home. It's about to implode.

It is evident that Elena favors her oldest child, seventeen-year-old daughter Lexie, who is the mirror image of her mother. Lexie is bold, controlling, and prudish with an air of self-importance. It also emerges that she is dishonest and a cheat. Her youngest daughter, fourteen-year-old Izzy, who Elena admits she never wanted, is nearly the opposite of her mother. She's honest, outspoken, and challenges Elena continually. As Izzy pushes back against her mother's strict rules and moralizing, a lot of ill feelings surface between the two. Izzy admits to her mother that she is gay only after everyone else in the family knows. While Lexie and Elena reflect each other, Izzy holds up a magnifying glass to her mother, which disrupts the woman's equilibrium. What stands out in Elena's mothering of Izzy is the deficit of maternal compassion and understanding. In one unforgettable and heartbreaking scene, the troubled girl is inconsolable in her bedroom one night after a fight with her mother. Izzy sees her mother's shadow under the door outside her room. Elena stands there for a few moments. Izzy looks hopeful that her mother will come in to talk, to comfort her or at least to reconnect. But her mother's shadow leaves. Elena is unable to bring herself to open the door and sit with her daughter. This painful scene can't help but make all of us confront our own similar experiences. It makes us squirm in our chairs. Those times when we as mothers are stubborn or unforgiving, when we could have done better. When we could have used lessons learned from our previous experiences. When we could have been wiser.

The contemporary views and narratives about mothering, which abound in all of our surrounding media, whether film, television, or personal interactions, are a primary focus of my work. *Little Fires Everywhere* dives into the complexities and complications of mothering. While we probably don't want to admit to it, we can all identify to some extent with Elena's character. She offers us a prime opportunity to examine the social and emotional constructs of motherhood, as a flawed human being, who, despite a respectable façade, reveals the underside of mothering—its unmentionable, unthinkable, taboo parts. They are sometimes on full display in her outward behavior, and at other times, they live below the surface. Elena manages to ignore these undesirable parts, perhaps out of fear that she isn't acceptable; or maybe because her real feelings are too much for her or her family to handle; or she may think that they must be buried away for her to keep moving forward. However, as is always the case in real life, this means that she's denying a real and genuine part of herself. Feelings cannot remain buried, nor can we find self-acceptance, kindness, or patience in denying our true emotions. While *Little Fires Everywhere* is fictitious and sometimes exaggerated, it reflects with unsettling honesty a part of life that we can relate to. Elena shows how blind we can be to our inner and outer worlds, how triggered we are by our children, and how deeply entrenched and automatic our responses to our children are. Her story demonstrates the importance of trying to understand this dynamic and recognize our own reactions so we can make meaningful change in our experience of motherhood. We also need to forgive ourselves more easily when we slip back into old habits.

As mothers, we're all familiar with the feeling of being emotionally triggered by our child and sometimes not being sure why. This may emerge in an argument, a moment of willful or rebellious behavior, a cranky attitude or tone of voice, which brings back past memories or familiar feelings of frustration or anger—toward your child or toward yourself or both. It can be so subtle that we are mostly unaware of what is going on. We may lose our cool, become overly sentimental or surprised, but we respond. Our children unconsciously know how to trigger us. They know where our vulnerabilities lie. And they press our buttons and keep pressing them. There is an ingenuity in the way that our child can do this. They hold up a mirror to us and we react.

When we as mothers can locate and reflect on the feelings and patterns that occur between ourselves and our children and the effect that we have on one another, we become more attuned and functional. This is one of the most complex and difficult undertakings in mothering. Elena's relationships with each of her daughters demonstrate this in such different ways. Lexie triggers the perfectionist side of Elena, the part of her who wants to believe everything is as it ought to be, whereas Izzy sets off her angry, judgmental, and insecure side. While Elena's reactions to both her daughters are opposite, neither are healthy. This illuminates the problems that come from limiting ourselves to only one kind of maternal feeling and experience with a child. When we assume our emotions will always be positive and expectations fulfilled, we deny so many other feelings and facets of ourselves and our children. At first glance, Elena and Lexie seem to have a close mother-and-daughter relationship, but it soon becomes apparent that Lexie has been encouraged to be Elena's buddy and her aide. Lexie fulfills the job of being Elena's reflection. She is the "good" daughter who is organized, who fits in, and who does what Elena considers to be the "right" things. This mutual devotion is really a toxic, if unconscious, pact between them, and Lexie pays a big price for being the favored child. She has to adjust her identity to conform to her mother's needs and expectations. Lexie is not free to be her own person, and Elena lives vicariously through her. The two are so dependent on each other for positive validation that Elena cannot countenance any imperfections in Lexie because that would destroy her faultless image of herself. Lexie is obligated to maintain this façade, which equally prohibits her from having flaws or making mistakes—she must be perfect. Their relationship is based on lies and superficiality.

When Lexie's life inevitably spirals out of control, she has no one to turn to. Unable to be truthful with her mother, she hides an abortion and cheats on her college entrance exam to get the good grades that Elena expects. It never occurs to Elena that the mutually caring, supportive, and validating interactions with her daughter are in fact erecting a wall between them. The pretext unravels in one of the last scenes, when Lexie confesses to her abortion and tells her mother that she isn't "fucking perfect," to which Elena screams, "Yes you are!" The girl's attempt to shed the burden that her mother has placed on her ends with Elena running back to her own bedroom and slamming the door, shutting herself off from Lexie.

Elena's dismissive, unkind, and volatile behavior toward Izzy is another extreme. To Elena, Izzy represents the "bad" girl who doesn't conform and is rebellious, outspoken, and argumentative. Izzy is charming, sassy, and marches to the beat of her own drum. She embarrasses Elena publicly. After a fight, Izzy refuses to play her violin part at the school concert. Instead, she sits motionless in her seat, with a message, "Not Your Puppet," written across her forehead, a message directed to Elena. Her mother cannot see Izzy for who she is because she is so preoccupied with her own expectations and reactions to her daughter's antics. Izzy is so much more than what is on the surface; she is caring and authentic, sensitive and generous, a highly intelligent girl who speaks her own truth. Elena cannot allow for the possibility that the feelings she experiences toward Izzy, including anger, shock, contempt, and unsteadiness, have anything to do with herself. However, as a mother and a professional in this area of motherhood, I suspect there is more to Elena's actions than meets the eye. While Izzy's behavior triggers outrage and shame in Elena, at a deeper level I believe that she may also symbolize Elena's own unfulfilled aspirations, someone that she wishes to be herself: Izzy, the free thinker, the one who can escape from, is uninhibited by, and contemptuous of social convention and isn't afraid to show it. Perhaps Izzy's constant challenge to her mother's strict rules reminds Elena that her life, and her notion of herself as the good girl, the good wife, and the good mother, depends on strict obedience to ideals and rules. Is Elena envious that Izzy feels free to be herself?

Elena cannot see either of her daughters in a full, realistic, and compassionate light, nor is she able to connect with the diverse feelings that each provokes in her, so instead she splits them into either the good or the bad child. She uses, in fact, one to reassure herself of her own perfection and the other to shield herself from her own shortcomings. She is incapable of seeing herself in the mirror that her daughters hold up to her, whether to use it as a red flag or to become curious about what it means for her mothering. Her inability to learn from her experiences marks an almost total lack of wisdom.

Even as adults, we often refuse to see the parts of ourselves we don't like or approve of, or we turn away in fear when we recognize our own traits on display in our children. Elena's rigid and excessive conduct toward her daughters makes us look at ourselves as moms: What is wise mothering? How do mothers cross the divide between the maternal ideal and reality? How do we create a space to talk about our struggles and to process and accept them rather than act on them? And, of course, we need to ask ourselves: How do we parent our different children? Are we fair? Do we treat them equally when the occasion calls for it and consider their unique differences? What do we do with the differing and multiple feelings that they set off in us?

In the final scenes of the series, there is a startling moment as Elena realizes that the responsibility for igniting all these little fires everywhere belongs to her. Her scheming attempts to hold her life together by controlling her environment give way to the shaky foundations of her seemingly picture-perfect life. Her previous reliance on secrecy and her divide-and-conquer mentality fail her, leaving her no choice but to grasp her truth and integrate all the parts of her life, everything that was previously separated between her inner and outer worlds. Her own image of herself as a good mother and an upright member of the community deteriorates as she recognizes in herself a deeply flawed character.

Elena's story reminds us that we all possess deeply biased psyches and that we need to be mindful of what we believe to be our own truth. It's often so much easier to create that inner fantasy world, where we get to choose to see things the way we want to, and we get to be oblivious to much of what is really going on around us—when we choose to talk rather than to listen, when we substitute the ideal for our authentic experiences, and when we emphasize intellectual prowess at the expense of learning from life experience.

But let's be careful not to fall into the trap of moralizing. Criticizing Elena's mothering means passing judgment on her failings and ignoring her many other strengths, as we all do with ourselves. Despite her shortcomings, she's not indifferent to her children; she struggles, and she worries. She does her best. On one occasion, she tells Izzy, "It's hard to be your mother"—and then these words are left hanging. There is no understanding or forgiving wise adult in the space to explore what this means. Despite her deficiencies, Elena has another side; we see snippets that display a softness, an ability to connect. In one moving scene, Izzy comes to her mother with a bleeding knee, and Elena gently tends to her by shaving her legs and putting a Band-Aid on her. However, once again the mother sabotages the moment, putting lipstick on Izzy and then uttering, "Perfect," her default position. This leaves Izzy, who remains staring at herself in the mirror, seemingly confused. Elena's tender gestures live together with her sense of entitlement, her self-righteousness, her lack of humor, and her inability to listen to and value what her children are saying to her. Mothering is a mosaic of experiences.

As much as we may judge and condemn Elena, her character offers us the opportunity to reflect on, to question, and to learn about our own mothering. Let's ask ourselves: What façades have we put in place for ourselves, for our children, perhaps even for the world? Are we also controlling, critical, and moralizing? Can we hear the truth about our children and our mothering, and if so, what do we do with it? Do we pay close attention to the deep contours of our mothering, or do we get caught up in the superficial? Are we able to be compassionate and forgiving of Elena, and by extension, of ourselves, for our maternal deficiencies? How do we manage our mismatches?

Elena's story reveals the taboos of mothering in their piercing and startling reality and is contrasted onscreen with the lives of other mothers, notably Mia, portrayed by Kerry Washington, a Black single mother who moves with her teenage daughter Pearl to the same small community. Mia is an artist, who up to this time has lived a nomadic existence with her daughter as she attempts to escape her secretive past. Despite difficult circumstances, including financial hardship and past trauma, mother and daughter have a close and warm connection, the polar opposite of Elena's financial comfort and her continual struggle with Izzy, the child she never really wanted and was never really able to claim.

Mia and Pearl have their fair share of parent-child strife, though. Pearl is showing signs of tiring of their nomadic lifestyle. She meets Moody, Elena's younger son, and quickly becomes seduced by his seemingly stable family life, with beautiful meals on the table and a mother who is at home. Pearl craves the dependability of a middle-class life, without the fear of poverty constantly lurking, while conversely, Izzy bathes in Mia's creativity and sense of freedom, her compassion and depth.

Unlike Elena, Mia is able to listen to and tolerate her daughter's complaints and anger toward her. She reflects and learns from them and is able to change. As Pearl begins to question her mother's choices, Mia recognizes her new reality. She must consider Pearl's words and let go a little so she doesn't lose her daughter. She fights to get the balance right between them, though she is able to understand that these difficult moments and confrontations, her discord and mismatches with Pearl, are an opportunity for growth, repair, and learning. Mia realizes that while she is the adult, she has a lot to learn from and about her daughter, and she will not always know what's best. Unlike Elena, who becomes more controlling as Izzy rebels, Mia checks her own rigidity. By learning to reflect rather than react, she is able to take a breath and choose fluidity and curiosity about her daughter's life rather than paralleling Pearl's behavior. It takes practice. While there are moments when she talks *at* rather than *to* Pearl, she learns from time and experience that this approach isn't going to work. So, she begins to integrate her intellect and her heart. She becomes a wiser mother.

Similar to the scene in which Izzy sees her mother's shadow under her door, an equally painful encounter unfolds between Mia and Pearl. After a massive confrontation, mother and daughter go to their own rooms. They have set up a special communication system when they sleep in their own rooms, knocking gently on the wall as a reminder of each other's presence and love and that everything is okay between them. Mia knocks on the wall—there is no sound. After some minutes of anguished silence, she hears her daughter's soft return knock. Mia sobs with relief as their connection is affirmed, renewed in this moment. Their relationship is one of repair as well as mutual tenderness and love.

At the end of the series, Elena and Mia must both face their own realities and their failures. This leads to the question that every honest mother asks herself at some point: Am I also a terrible mother?

There is no straight answer to this question, which is full of shades and combinations. Perhaps we can start with the reality that at times I am a terrible mother, and at other times I am a wonderful mother. Can we live with and reach this truth—the ambivalence of our motherhood?

To draw on *Little Fires Everywhere*, sometimes we are Elena, and sometimes we are Mia. Our wisdom lies in being aware of who we are from moment to moment, replacing our judgments with an acceptance of imperfection and adapting the lessons from past experience to the present, and to the days, weeks, months, and years ahead. Elena and Mia both have faults and strengths, embodying most mothers who are trying to do their best. The greatest thing they—and others, including ourselves—can teach us is that at any stage of mothering, no matter how late, we can gain some wisdom in admitting our mistakes and repairing rather than burying them. Our relationships with each of our children are unique, provoking distinct feelings and reactions in us and requiring us to be different mothers to each. The mismatches and discord are a valuable opportunity to learn about ourselves and our children. By understanding and valuing the different parts of ourselves, we can become more grounded and humane mothers. Recognizing the ideal for what it is, and undoing some of our entrenched beliefs about it, leads us to wisdom.

There are a multitude of mothering experiences that we cannot face, that are too dangerous to even think about, much less verbalize. Elena's startling admission that she never really wanted Izzy opens one of the most taboo discussions imaginable. After bottling up her true feelings for years, Elena explodes in a rage at the end of the series, revealing the secret that she's been holding inside for years, the cause of all the little fires everywhere, which cannot be extinguished. In this moment, she is possessed by a seething, unutterable rage, nearly choked by her pent-up emotions. She is out of control, in a state that has no name. Is it despair, sadness, fear? There seems to be something inside her that is buried so deep, and is so frightening, that she cannot communicate or reach it. Instead, she allows it to live in a place that will potentially destroy her. This decision, conscious or not, won't encourage space for the ebb and flow of love or room for reflection and dialogue to infiltrate.

How do we begin to unpack Elena's disturbing truth? She isn't able to make the connection between never really wanting a fourth child and how it has affected her relationship with Izzy. Izzy's identity is deeply influenced by the truth that her mother has felt trapped by her presence from the beginning.

Elena is by far not the first woman to have a baby she didn't want. Like some women in real life, she accidentally became pregnant as she was just starting to resume some independent, normal life after having three babies in quick succession. Fourteen years later, when the series begins, Elena's heartbreaking regret has transformed into a dynamic that affects her entire family.

This is the ultimate taboo subject when it comes to motherhood and to maternal ambivalence. Is it okay for a mother to not want her baby? And what happens when a mother has her baby amid those doubts? While the questions of a right to life and abortion are perennial and pernicious hot-button topics, what I'm talking about here is so much harder in ways for women to discuss—it's not dinner-table discussion but rather whispered gossip or confession. Perhaps if Elena had a space—and more crucially, permission—to talk about and process her feelings honestly, rather than bottling them up, her situation might have been different.

Leaning into these taboo feelings and questions, while seemingly counterintuitive, can teach us so much about ourselves as mothers and why our maternal ideals are so closely tethered to the myths and rules that have kept us both paralyzed and moving frantically in the wrong direction. Elena's fixed ideas about what's right prevent her from recognizing that value exists in conflicting and upsetting feelings. I suspect that if Elena had given herself permission to connect with her honest feelings about Izzy, as taboo and wrong as they felt, she would have been a different mother to Izzy and to the rest of her children. Had she understood the danger of so strictly observing societal pressure, often at the cost of her authentic feelings, she would most likely have been more able to access and tolerate her more difficult ones. Perhaps she could have been more compassionate and forgiving of both herself and her daughter, and less angry and resentful. Certainly, if she had faced her feelings over the years, she might have avoided such an agonizing scene for Izzy. In contradiction to contemporary and age-old beliefs, our acknowledgment of troubling feelings does not hinder our mothering, because they speak the truth. Above all, naming our feelings normalizes them.

Elena's meltdown and its meaning are so worthy of reflection, of the dueling messages that lie at the root of mothering. On one hand, it's acceptable to show how flawed you are; on the other, being honest means you'll never get to be the ideal mother. By uttering her truth, Elena enters into dangerous but not uncharted waters. The notion that a mother does not want her child is so startling and so socially repugnant. But what do we do with it? Are we able to both blame her for the fires and to have some empathy and understanding for her? Or do we discard her because we cannot bear to hear these words, which are also a cry for help? Her confession, that she symbolically ignited the little fires everywhere, marks the culmination of the previous disastrous chain of events and Elena's confounding and honest moment of reconciliation—her moment of truth. There is still hope. Pushed to the edge, Elena reaches self-awareness and self-acceptance. She names her ambivalence.

Little Fires Everywhere touches on so much of what is mothering: the taboo parts, the burden of social and personal expectations, the never-ending days, and the routine ordinary life with our children. Elena's story teaches us, surprises us, shocks us. It is a commentary on what inhibits us and what liberates us. It forces us to ask whether we value all aspects of our mothering, whether we integrate our myriad conflicting feelings—our joy, our pain, our motherlove, our resentments, our anger, our joy, our tenderness, and our ordinary, fleeting flashes of hate—into an overall acceptance of who we are and who our children need us to be.

SIX

MOTHERING UNHINGED

IN *LITTLE FIRES EVERYWHERE,* ELENA experiences what I refer to as "mothering on the edge" when her world comes tumbling down, her identity plunging into disarray. She has a realization, she takes responsibility for her actions and their effects, and she shrugs off some of her impossible ideals as all of her feelings integrate into her most genuine self. Her meltdown comes with a lightning bolt.

Psychologist and author of *Maternal Desire*, Daphne de Marneffe,[61] names the unpleasant feelings that emerge in relation to one's children as the place "where the real human work gets done, where the emotional action is."[62] Let's face it—as moms, we can become unhinged when something totally knocks us off balance, when life with our children just gets to be too much, and we feel like we're simply spinning out of control. Unforgettable times of extraordinary challenge can be momentary or lingering. There are periods that bring staggering losses, pain, and disruptions to our daily life. The tough times are not what we signed up for—they defy most of our expectations. It's too much. Inner conflict erupts as we're forced to reconcile our daily reality with our thwarted dreams. We feel stuck in those circumstances, and there are days when it's a struggle to believe life will get better, that we'll ever be happier, beyond that bleak moment. Our feelings of shame fuel that sense of disbelief, dragging us down even further. These are the moments that, any mother will attest, change us forever, though at the time, it's impossible to make sense of them, to talk about them in any meaningful way, or to make peace with them—so we silence them. This is mothering on the edge.

Usually the drama passes, and we steady ourselves, and we get on with our lives fairly quickly. But what happens when something disrupts the mother's life so totally that it doesn't go back into place, and she is forced to confront her new reality? When the gap between her dreams and reality is so wide that it can no longer be crossed? For some of us, this means finding a way to survive—getting to the end of an hour, a day, a month, or a year until we find our equilibrium again. When we're forced to dig deep and lean into those raw experiences, we can learn a lot from, and about, ourselves as mothers. The wise mother begins to realize that the maternal ideals and the silence she's held onto previously are no longer working for her. As the myths and ideals are broken apart, the silences that previously shielded her are revealed as empty. She understands that they cannot guard her from her overwhelming barrage of unbearable feelings.

In fact, we really cannot begin to understand the reality of everyday mothering without considering this dark and troubling underside, because it is inevitable that life with your children will bring on these moments of sheer sorrow and hopelessness, even though they most often pass. Mothering on the edge opens up this discussion. Do any of these words from new mothers sound familiar to you?

"I returned home and everything looked different. I was different. I was a mother, but I had no idea how to be a mother."

"She smiles at me. She loves me unconditionally and absolutely. The purity of her emotions takes my breath away."

"We stumble through the first phase of motherhood feeling lost, trying to will the fog away."

"What am I doing wrong? Because I feel like I'm doing everything wrong."

"There's no room in my life for me."

"I just felt so alone on the island of motherhood."

"My life was completely turned upside down over a small human I wasn't even sure I liked, let alone felt anything maternal toward."

"None of it—not the books or the showers or the childbirth classes—prepared me to understand my new role or revealed my new self to the larger society. All I had in my toolkit were useless platitudes: You'll be fine! Rely on your mother's intuition! You'll just know!"

"Once I got past my fear of not feeling what I thought I should feel, and gave myself permission to love at my own pace, some of the guilt and panic abated. I wish someone had reached out to me and validated the way I was feeling."

These ordinary voices sound so familiar, describing our everyday sensations of mothering. The joy, the loneliness, the trepidation, and the reality of these feelings can occur together in one instant, in one day, or over many days. However, there is something about them that is unexpected. They are part of a collection of stories from *Mothering Through the Darkness*,[63] edited by Stephanie Sprenger and Jessica Smock. The quotes come from mothers, many of whom are writers, who have recovered from postpartum depression. Their stories are primarily from their early days of mothering and give voice to the heart-wrenching struggle between love and what mothers often experience in their most vulnerable moments of despondency, recovery, and renewal.

Mothering on the edge teaches us about what we can do when we are really pushed to the brink of something unexpected. There are many mothers who haven't gone through postpartum depression. So, is this relevant to everyday mothering? Definitely. Postpartum depression holds a special, if distinctly separate, place in the mothering experience because it warrants particular research and consideration, but equally, it reminds us of everyday mothering thrown into its sharpest relief. It's one of the most powerful examples of the emotional overwhelm that can hit us when least expected, bring us to our knees in doubt and unhappiness, and then suddenly lift like a cloud and be gone in weeks or months, leaving us to wonder how it could possibly have been real. It is real, and the doubts and the trauma live forever inside a mom, even as she feels the joy when the light finally comes through. The intensity of the postpartum life has motivated these women to freely speak of their taboo feelings and experiences, even those feelings of hatred. They speak of what is generally hidden and silenced: painful and distressing experiences that need compassion and understanding. And they normalize our experiences of mothering, what we are all trying to survive every day. They offer us hope, but more important, they offer us a language that helps us to speak of our own maternal anguish as part of our love. Their words help us to see our realities more clearly and show us that we are not spectators. Their stories belong to all of us to some degree or another. We can learn from these experiences.

Postpartum depression is, to be very clear, a condition that can be so severe as to require medical intervention and treatment, and women who suffer from it are not just having a bad day. It is one of the most extreme examples of mothering on the edge. It has the sense of being thrown into a totally unexpected place, falling down a rabbit hole at warp speed. Expectations, rules, and rigidity are all challenged, and often there is just survival. Mothers who can articulate their pain and volunteer their stories strike a deep chord. In *Mothering Through the Darkness*, some mothers are honest and brave enough to confess their hating feelings toward their children. Here lies my enigma: Did the mother's capacity to name her hating feelings help her recovery, or had she reached such depths of despair that her brutal truth was free to just come tumbling out? I'm not sure that one or the other is the only answer, but these admissions allow all of us to step into another territory. Every time one mother opens up and makes use of these feelings in everyday conversation, more of us are able to identify ourselves with her and admit what it is we all truthfully think and feel. I'm not claiming that every mother has hateful feelings or moments, but I am encouraging mothers to find and use their own words to name their difficult feelings and to value them. The truth of these feelings shapes, rather than undoes, one's mothering.

I'm curious about these more lingering experiences, which change a mother's life to such a degree that she has to somehow adjust to the tsunami that has hit her. From the get-go, these wise moms quickly realize what exceptional mothering requires. They are confronted with their uncomfortable feelings, and yet they understand the frailty of the maternal ideal. I'm curious about how these experiences somehow bring out something robust, courageous, and empowering for the mother and what this can teach us about our mothering. The extreme examples can be a path toward understanding our motherhood. We can discover so much from the stories of mothers who fight for their children's best interests and their own identities amid the most challenging times—times when a mother has to rely on her resilience, her bravery, and her instincts to protect and look after her child, no matter her own emotional or physical state. It soon becomes obvious that the myths, taboos, and ideals of mothering are unsustainable—they block flow and truth.

These are the mothers who show up every day to build and maintain the relationship with their child, often against enormous odds.

I'm reminded of Joh, whose new motherhood was almost immediately defined by the onset of Bell's palsy, a facial paralysis that prevented her from smiling, blinking, tasting food, or speaking without slurring. In an article published online on March 26, 2021, by The Grace Tales Team,[64] and in conversation with me, Joh described her fear and heartache as she waited in terror and longing for her face, which she no longer recognized as her own, to return to normal. Joh was plunged into mothering on the edge, not knowing whether her paralysis would be temporary or permanent. Would she ever be able to return her baby's first smile?

Joh's first weeks of motherhood immediately called into question some of the most basic tenets of the maternal ideal. She confronted the accepted beliefs of what a mother is expected to do, not to mention the notion of the selfless, all-giving mother. She admitted later, with a tinge of bitter humor, that she'd wondered honestly about what a new mother who barely knows her baby should be expected to give up, and how much of herself, and whether that could "reasonably include my face?" She was brave enough to prioritize her own well-being at the time, putting on her "own mask first" in her words, and made part of her mothering "about herself" in addition to her baby. Joh leaned into her trauma by engaging in it, looking for ways to keep herself afloat while she wiled away the time, willing her face to return. She passed the hours watching mindless television, late night internet shopping while feeding her baby, and waiting. Throughout the ordeal, she was patient, thoughtful, and clear about the help she was willing to ask for and accept from others, which included practical help from selected family and friends and medication. She now recounts memorable words from a wise woman who assured her that, in time, "either your circumstances will change or you will adjust."

While Joh is addressing new mothers in her article, her words send a resounding and powerful message to moms at all stages. She advocates for other mothers in the postpartum period by acknowledging the difficulties that new motherhood can bring. She is enthusiastic about sharing her story and encourages an openness and honesty about mothering. "I learnt a few lessons about resilience, conviction and the fragility of postnatal mental health. As no woman seems to come out of pregnancy or childbirth unscathed, I share these lessons here in the hope that it helps other women who are looking to pick up their pieces, however they have been scattered." Her capacity to normalize the struggles that new mothers face, to find the space to actively yet patiently wait while questioning her concerns, to challenge the maternal ideal, and to help others in her situation is inspiring. Her words reveal the creativity and flexibility that is needed for any mother to propel herself through the many unknowns that mothering will keep presenting. Joh leaves us with a lot to absorb from her vulnerability and strength. She is open and clear about her pain and empowers herself through her endurance and insistence on finding ways to soften her suffering. Her description of mothering as an experience that we all "muddle" through speaks the truth.

Adopting a child is another example of mothering on the edge. I've spoken with adoptive mothers who tell me about their experiences, including feeling untethered by their emotions, the overturning of daily life, the impact of their difference from biological moms, and the comments and judgments from others. They learn that in order to survive, they need to minimize their expectations of other people and find creative ways to reach their own agency and build their resilience.

Clara adopted her son Jason when he was five months old. She felt enormous love immediately for him but also recounts the stress of being thrown into the foreign space of motherhood. In addition to the usual struggles that most new mothers experience, such as difficulty in settling the baby, Clara also felt the extra pressure of having to be the "best" mom because she was bringing up someone else's child. She felt scared about doing the "wrong things" and fell prey to a lot of doubts about herself as a mother, often questioning whether in fact she should have become one. She tells the story of attending a group for new mothers and babies, suddenly struck by the realization that while the other mothers had a history with their baby, she had missed the first months of Jason's life. She felt lonely and disconnected in a way that she found difficult to name. She tries to explain the feeling: "These moms had their babies in their bellies from the beginning, and they had a 'knowing' about their baby" that she felt she was missing. Mundane comments from others such as, "You are so lucky to have a baby," and, "It must be like it was a dream come true," upset her because she sensed something condescending in their tone that reinforced her fear that she was different, less of a mother perhaps. She wondered, "Surely everyone must feel grateful to have a baby, or is it just me who must give total and unending thanks? Am I entitled to be unhappy even a minute of the day?" This was compounded by the fact that motherhood was unexpectedly hard work; she felt that she had no right to have, much less express, her sadness, anger, and exhaustion. She also felt confused, because of course she was the luckiest woman in the world to have a baby like Jason. But there were days when...

In time, she found a group of adoptive moms who allowed her to be honest about the reality of her days and her feelings, to talk about the monotonous, dreadful, and wonderful parts of being a mom. Clara noticed that when she was able to open up, what she describes as "a cone of silence" that adoptive mothers have around their mothering, this gave permission for all of the moms in the group to do the same, which bolstered her own confidence. But more important, Clara found the right sympathetic ear—parents who were going through similar struggles—allowing her to begin to shed the guilt and shame that came from both outside comments and her own doubts and fears. We are never alone in our experience, a vital lesson for anyone regardless of circumstance. No matter what maternal conflict you're feeling, someone out there is feeling it too.

The life story of Lucy and her adopted daughter Sammy demonstrates that mothering on the edge can keep reemerging over a lifetime. As a little girl, Sammy was delightful, but by the time she turned eight, she was showing signs of being troubled. She had South American olive skin and was painfully self-conscious of not being fair like the other girls. She was aware of being a perpetual outsider and foreigner; everything was difficult for her and around her, and Lucy took the brunt. When Sammy was fifteen, she became pregnant. Because of her own experience of being adopted and abandoned, the girl could not reconcile an abortion or the thought of giving her child away. So the young teenager left school, had her baby Marny, and remained at home with Lucy, who took over the primary care of both granddaughter and daughter.

During my conversation with Lucy, I was alerted to a deeper level of meaning that the impact of mothering on the edge holds. Mothering is practiced in part across the generations—for better (and sometimes for worse) we learn from our mothers and often imitate them with our children. Her own family's intergenerational pattern of trauma and loss soon became apparent to Lucy. She was squeezed between a mother and teenage daughter who both faced considerable mental health issues and who were both adoptees, abandoned by their birth mothers at some stage in their child-hood. Lucy has a deep and wonderful connection with her granddaughter Marny, who she describes lovingly as "a new soul." She also knows only too well the heartache that dealing with an emotionally unwell mother brings and that at some level Marny is at risk. While mothering both her teenage daughter and granddaughter at the same time is a big undertaking, she willingly signs up for it with an open heart.

Lucy made an interesting comment that I have been thinking about. While she knows that her granddaughter has been exposed to much struggle in her short life, Lucy feels buoyed up by the incredible amount of love that surrounds Marny. The little girl has a mother who, while no doubt unwell, loves her deeply. She also has an involved and loving father and caring grandparents on both sides. Lucy expresses much more concern about her daughter Sammy. Her experience of mothering on the edge is rooted in the persistent worry that "I know I cannot fix it for her," or, I add, for herself. Her tone was despairing with a tinge of acceptance.

As I was talking to Lucy, I noted another parallel process. Lucy holds a fear of someday being abandoned herself by her own daughter, so it seems that Lucy's mothering on the edge is intensified by the possibility of another generational repetition. Despite Lucy's pain and concern about this and the disruption to her own daily life that her daughter brings, she has found agency in acknowledging the reality. She keeps moving forward and resists becoming stuck. She cannot repair her daughter, and the only control she actually has is, ironically, in her acceptance that she really has no control over her own or her daughter's life or the future.

Lucy's story reminds me that we often bring loss, along with the rest of our psychic baggage, into our new relationships, and bringing it into motherhood is no different. When I met Katy, she was mother to three children, an eighteen-, fifteen-, and eleven-year-old, and had struggled with her youngest child, Jake, compared to the fairly straightforward raising of her other children. She attributed this to personality differences, her own more advanced age, and the closer ages between her older two, which made them natural playmates. As she recounted the stories of her mothering since the birth of her youngest, something suddenly struck her. Her mothering of Jake had become very difficult when the little boy was about three, which she realized coincided with the exact time that her beloved brother had been diagnosed with cancer. Until Jake was about ten, she'd been fully immersed in her brother's treatment and then her grief at his death. The aftermath of his passing was almost as harrowing as the previous years, and Katy took a long time to process its meaning. The feelings of sorrow and anguish at the loss of her brother, together with her everyday life, moved her to mothering on the edge. Until our exchange, it had been too painful for her to consciously make a connection between the profound impact of her brother's death and her fractured relationship with Jake. It was now becoming increasingly clear to Katy that for many of his formative years, she hadn't been emotionally present for her son, and a cycle of dysfunctional behavior had evolved between the two of them. As Jake's demands for his mother's time and attention grew, she retreated from him, and the more emotionally absent she was, the needier he became. She was able to see that she had let her little boy down in not being present for him. And in this light-bulb moment, she was faced with reopening the wound from her brother's passing, amplified by her truth that she had failed her son. She was momentarily stuck between a rock and a hard place, torn in two by guilt, because for Katy, holding onto one meant abandoning the other. As she reached what seemed to her as the very edge of her mothering capacity, a kind of inner reconciliation and fluidity was also gathering. She had no choice but to acknowledge that while she couldn't bring her brother back, she had a child who needed and wanted her love profoundly. By giving herself permission to let go of her grief, she was free to return slowly to her mothering. She set aside a few hours each week when she could "be with" and reminisce about her brother, and her fear of abandoning or forgetting him abated. This gave her the peace and renewed sense of agency to devote to Jake and to restore balance to her life.

Little Fires Everywhere starkly portrays these common feelings of frenzy and hopelessness that occur every day for mothers. The episode "The Uncanny"[65] shows a flashback to the experience of Elena and the difficulty she has settling and feeding Izzy as a baby. The household is in an uproar with three other children running around, and Elena is desperate to quiet her infant. When she turns on the tap to fill her baby's bottle, she discovers that the water in the house has been turned off because of an unpaid bill. She totally loses control. She calls her husband and abuses him. She smashes plates on the floor. When her husband arrives home, with bottled water, to the chaotic scene, Elena throws the baby at him and escapes into the night. Her anger, loneliness, and helplessness are piercing.

A similarly agonizing experience emerges for Bebe, played by Huang Lu, a single mother who is an illegal immigrant in the USA and is also trying to feed her screaming baby. In episode three, called "Seventy Cents,"[66] the desperate mother goes to the store to buy some formula, but she is seventy cents short, and the cashier cruelly shoos her out, refusing to help. At this point, Bebe sees no solution. As an illegal immigrant, she cannot ask for social support, as this would risk deportation, and yet her baby needs food. She is so distraught that she abandons her child on the doorstep of a fire station.

While these two vignettes are from television, they represent real-life experiences and are an acute reminder of the complete torment and desolation that some moments of mothering bring, and of both the universality and the uniqueness of every mother's experience. Joyce Edward throws light on these experiences by naming the "intact"[67] mother as one who can provide basic economic and environmental necessities of life for her child. She adds that these are crucial to any mother's ability to care for her child, physically and mentally. Watching the series helps us to keep in mind that some mothers are unable to access these needed resources and opens our eyes to the reality that many mothers exist in bleak and disadvantaged economic and social environments, which understandably push them to a breaking point. As the series unfolds, we are forced to continually reflect on how a mother's social and economic circumstances, as well as her individual qualities and those of her child, all impact her life. This speaks to how unfair this can be for some women, our need for compassion, and the truth of the statement: "There, but for the grace of G-d, go I."

There are stories of mothering on the edge that are true outliers, those that we cannot conceive of happening to anyone, least of all ourselves. But they are the stories that prove that everyday miracles exist, that offer evidence of our endless capacity for love in the face of tragedy and our resilience as mothers in even our darkest hours. In 2017, Tatjana Takseva, journalist, writer, and professor of a broad range of studies in the area of women and gender studies, published a paper[68] about her research of a small number of Bosnian women who made the decision to bear their children born of wartime rape by Serbian soldiers.

Takseva recounts the experience of Jasmina, one of the young mothers, who was much more open than most mothers can be around their taboo feelings, saying that she "had to work very hard to love my child."[69] She experienced intense mood swings in the early months and years of motherhood and described moments when she was tormented by her daughter's demanding cries, the baby's angry face reminding Jasmina of her rapist. Her ability to manage these incidents by giving herself time out demonstrates an unusual sense of creative thinking and resourcefulness. Jasmina was also able to distinguish her shifting moods and feelings, knowing that her negative emotions were offset by her strong commitment to look after and love her child and to keep herself and her life intact. Despite very difficult circumstances, Jasmina could clearly and bravely name her struggles with her child. Knowing the source of her maternal ambivalence granted her a legitimate space in which to claim it, and yet the complexity of her feelings is expressed in her admission that she credits her daughter as being the one who helped her to return "back to some sort of normality"[70] despite her harrowing experiences.

Safeta, another rape victim, tells a not dissimilar story. After initially rejecting her son and placing him in an orphanage, she realized after six months that she couldn't live without him. It was enormously difficult to persuade the authorities to return her child to her, though she triumphed eventually. She states, "If I hadn't found him when I did, I probably wouldn't be alive now."[71] A vision that they would be reunited became "the sole purpose of her living."[72] Safeta also expressed feelings of relief that she'd had a boy rather than a girl, who may have faced the same fate as hers. When discussing the haunting question of keeping a child whose father represented the enemy, she said, "I didn't care less what others thought."[73]

What these women had to say about motherhood on the edge is far, far more easily said than done, and each of them paid an enormous price before and after their decisions to raise their children. Both women faced family pressures and wider social judgment in response to their choices. The war between countries and cultures, and the enemy, was brought right inside peoples' homes, both literally and metaphorically. Jasmina and Safeta were able to disentangle themselves, for the most part, from the usual expectations placed on mothers, which granted them in some ways a special sympathy and compassion. By freeing themselves from the typical ideals of mothering, they could work through their complicated emotions, connecting immediately and honestly with maternal taboos. This tells us something about what we don't often allow ourselves to do as mothers—to seize any opportunity to repair our emotional landscape and reconnect with our child—and that we must find some light in the dark. We can do more than merely survive.

These are but a few of the infinite mothering stories. There are countless others, and any reader will no doubt find one or two to relate to: There is the mother whose baby spends the first ten weeks of life in NICU.[74] The newly immigrated or displaced mother. The mother who misses her own mother desperately through death, distance, or estrangement. The mother whose child is missing or gone, either in reality or emotionally. The mother of a child with significant emotional or physical challenges. The mother who has gone through previous reproductive losses, such as infertility, miscarriage, or stillbirth. The mother suffering from the trauma of abortion and its aftershocks. The mother who loses her partner and raises her child alone. Gay and single-parent households. And of course, the working mother, who hardly sees her children, versus the homemaker mother stuck with them all day, both trying valiantly to achieve the right balance, to navigate the alternate feelings of abandonment and freedom.

All these experiences, no matter whether a mother is raising her child with a partner or by herself, are compounded by fear—of failure, of losing her child, of losing herself. Naming our feelings, finding that first step forward, allows us to begin shedding those fears. Acknowledging that mothering is, from the beginning, an experience of discord, as well as love, marked by dilemmas, turmoil, and doubts, does away with so many unnecessary illusions: the possibility of perfect union with one's child—being a wholly caring, constantly available, and unconditionally loving mother.

This has to be an active process. Our struggles shape us and allow us to accept and work with, rather than neglect, the pain and shame of our experiences, and then to assign a meaning and words to them. Each of the women I've interviewed or researched overcame difficult circumstance by leaning into her experiences rather than avoiding them and by demonstrating a capacity to think through a painful situation, to name the variety of her emotions, and to make discernible choices and decisions that changed the course of her relationship with her child and with herself. Their brave voices tell us that getting through extraordinary experiences means enduring much suffering, knowing that while they cannot control their situations, they can control their reactions, some days. This empowers them. This is their wisdom.

SEVEN

SHOWING UP EVERY DAY

OUR SOCIAL AND CULTURAL UNDERSTANDING of maternal love is difficult to put into words. By giving it a name, "motherlove," I can more easily draw its shape and capture the nuances and contours of the feelings that go with it. Motherlove is a special balancing and maternal energy that is shaped unconsciously by the mother. Motherlove has seconds, maybe minutes, of purity. While motherlove is sometimes sentimental and romantic, this is not its mainstay. It's more complicated and real than that. Love in any of its truest definitions is by no means a uniform, smooth, or level emotion. It undulates; it grows; it ebbs and flows with continual mismatching and correction. It doesn't bear indifference, or a cutting-off, but it tolerates maternal ambivalence, as dark and distressing moments and taboo feelings breathe oxygen into a mother's love for her child.

Motherlove is the central element of the mother's experience from which all other maternal feelings flow, whether they contain joy or pain. The mother's ability to stay and struggle with her troubling feelings, as they fuel and nourish her love, is the face of maternal ambivalence. Maternal ambivalence is founded on the idea of *and*: sadness *and* happiness, love *and* despair. It shuns the exclusivity of *or*, such as tenderness *or* pain, suffering *or* joy, by upholding that both exist together. It does not tolerate the judgment that the word "should" provokes. A mother's ability to achieve maternal ambivalence is a sign of her emotional well-being.

There is often an uneasy fit between crucial moments of elation, where there is rhythm and flow and mutual nourishment, and the more frequent moments, where everyday problems, difficulties, and routine reside. Motherlove has an inner voice that allows a mother to rally her loving feelings and to nestle and calm her distressing emotions so she can care for her child and for herself. By being in the moment and connecting with her feelings as fully as she can and not neglecting the ones that are uncomfortable, she grows as a mother. This is the reality of motherlove.

On a good day, motherlove is unparalleled in its tenacity. It has a short memory. It is forgiving. It is aware of the pitfalls of judgment and expectation; it is flowing; it questions itself without moralizing. It provides a nest in which to hold and respect distressing feelings, to renew and transform them. It is curious about these dark moments but does not brush them away or become contaminated by them; rather, it inspires and enables us to find meaning in them. It understands that when we strip our feelings to their basics, there are loving moments and there are also hating moments, or feelings akin to them but perhaps not named as such, and these are tied together—the intensity and passion of each fuels the other. They exist together and are continually in motion. This is maternal ambivalence.

The enduring theme in this book is the presence of motherlove and its capacity to both nestle and fuel the mothers' distressing feelings—her anger, her resentment, and her hating flashes. Naming her difficult feelings helps the mother to lean into her mothering and its unknowns. While it seems counterintuitive, censoring her distressing feelings actually moves her back into the space of ideals and rigidity when she needs to remain fluid. The stories that I recount, drawn from personal experience, film, and television, teach us lessons about motherlove and all the other emotions that mothering brings to the table. They cast a magnifying glass on motherhood and cause us to rethink how mothering is viewed and understood, as Takseva says, to redefine her "motherlove in terms that are empowering to mothers."[75] The influence of maternal expectations figures deeply, and these stories examine these taboos and their purpose. Thought needs to be given to the value that arises from the tension of conflicting feelings sitting together and how hard it is for the mother to freely reflect on and express her shameful and powerful feelings. Let's remove the masks from mothers, see them as they are, and learn from them.

Any real discussion of mothering places the idea of ambivalence, the coexistence of our conflicting feelings, at the center of the conversation. While we gush about the beauty, meaning, and joys of mothering, by its very nature, this typically close constant connection also holds an underside that bears uncomfortable and silenced truths. These dark feelings, tensions, and messiness continue to shock and surprise us, even as they are an everyday part of our life as mothers with its challenges and conflicts. A dynamic tension surfaces between our loving and troubling feelings—which, rather than threatening or compromising our love, become a source of learning and healing. Our ambivalent feelings thrive on connection as spurts of love, tenderness, pity, and longing manage to coexist with patches of disappointment, revulsion, frustration, and many more feelings, inspiring us to keep moving forward. Despite the discomfit of outer expectations and our inner turmoil, we manage to show up every day to mother the best way we can.

Being stirred up by our children is a normal part of being a mom. The question is what do we do with these feelings? Holding onto these feelings of ambivalence is not so easy. Sometimes it's just too much, and instead of staying engaged with our disturbing feelings, we revert back to our rigid ways. We try to block our pain, and perhaps we turn to social expectations to guide us. But in the long run, this just doesn't work. When we can accept and live with these contradictions and challenges, rather than trying to control or neglect them, this brings us to the best spot to repair and heal from the bruises of mothering. Our struggles are valuable and bring dramatic internal transformation. We experience the magic of maternal ambivalence.

My own mothering history has its foundations in birthing a new baby in three different decades: I gave birth to a child in my twenties, in my thirties, and in my forties. This experience has taken me on a meandering track of starts and stops in motherhood and has certainly provided me with a lifetime of backstories, side routes, and learning opportunities along the way. My path has led through challenges and hard-earned lessons, with unexpected obstacles to climb over that helped me to understand, eventually, the dynamics of mothering and set me on the course to write this book. When I ponder my mothering experiences, some phrases and words come to my mind: the ebbs and flows, the bittersweet and despairing, the pushes and pulls. Over time, I learned to accept the rocky path and lean into the flow—its shocks, uphill moments, and delights.

My work continually forces me to think back on my own experiences and feelings as a mother, my failures and my triumphs. It provokes all the questions that relate to how we live as mothers today. What makes us tick? What vitalizes and nourishes us? What holds us back? How do we find our voice?

I gave birth first at age twenty-three, then at thirty-two, and finally again at forty-one. I've described myself at times as a young mother, a middle-aged mother, and an older mother. People often stared at me quizzically or wondered aloud about the age gap. Some would ask: The same father? How can you stand going back to nappies? Is it like having three only children? While I might surprise some people when I mention the age gap between my children, I in turn marvel at how other moms manage the fighting and competition between their more closely spaced children and their ability to balance their time so they can dedicate enough to each child. As the Rolling Stones' Mick Jagger wisely tells us, we can't always get what we want—but we do get what we need.

My three somewhat separate mothering experiences have shown me many new and surprising things about myself. Each stage has been so different, and as I shifted from being a young new mother to an older one, my priorities, expectations, and insights also changed. I often think about my own mothering map, how and why it played out for me the way it did, and I wonder about the impact of significant occurrences in my life. By recounting my own personal experiences, I'm hoping that it will also encourage my readers to reflect on how they themselves were mothered and how they mother their children as they learn more about themselves and the messages of value that they have gathered.

At twenty-three, I was a young, naïve, and loving mother. I gave birth just over a year after leaving home and getting married. It's now so clear to me that at that age I was, to put it lightly, ill-equipped to face the struggles that confronted me. Funnily enough, my unworldliness also brought resources of vitality, innocence, and energy that served me well—youth definitely helps there. As the years unfolded, and I passed through the mothering cycle, I became more fluid and surrendered more to the fluctuations of daily life, and I was able to be more accepting of the notion that "it will be what it will be."

Without questioning it, I relied on that early, unwritten but familiar rule book: be the good mother, above all else. The underlying messages that were transmitted to me included: put your children first, be physically present, be reliable, and be stubbornly independent. Life revolved around my baby and the family, and I was stuck between the two in a 1950s model of divided roles. I hadn't managed to find a comfortable space in which to understand and voice my true range of feelings and difficulties and fulfill some of my own needs while balancing what my baby needed from me. With hindsight, I almost always assumed that I had to have all the answers myself, a fairly rigid approach. This undermined my ability to appreciate the flow and openness that mothering requires and the value of questioning my life. I was generally stuck in the mode of acting the way I thought I was supposed to while struggling with the inner emotional conflict provoked by feelings of loneliness and my new identity, which often surfaced in the form of whether I could work outside the home and be a fully engaged mom. Mom life was sometimes so confusing, often I felt like I just couldn't figure out how to get things right. I was not making sense of what can be learned from real-life experiences. Sometimes my head and heart were in dialogue and other times not. However, I loved my child deeply and most of the time loved being a mother.

When I ask myself today what I had imagined as a first-time mother, I believe that I was yearning for an experience of pure love, bliss, and connection, one that would complete me. Most likely this fantasized union with my child would heal something missing for me; it carried the hope that being a mother would be my path at last to real truth and meaning. The reality is that I didn't have a clue about what mothering meant, but I started with an open, generous heart—not bad credentials. And I really wanted to be a mom. However, it wasn't until I let go of the perfectionist fantasy and experienced some mothering on the edge and truth about my everyday life that I could begin to build a narrative to understand myself as a mother.

As far as everyday life went, my newborn son and I adapted easily to each other, and most of the time we were in sync. I didn't experience some of the early difficulties that many new mothers have. I didn't see the need to stress unduly about certain circumstances. When my milk supply waned at four weeks, I tried to build it up for two weeks, and when that didn't work, I made the decision to stop breastfeeding. I suppose I had a steely resolve coupled with acceptance, which I credit to the upside of youth and innocence. Breastfeeding wasn't my thing, my baby had to thrive, and he needed food, so it was simple.

Sometimes I was on autopilot, and at other times I had "wow" moments of deep learning and wisdom. I felt an almost mysterious connection with my baby from the first day of his life. I woke up from my sleep at almost the same second he did, though he was in the nursery, not lying next to me. I felt a consolidation of purpose, a vindication that this was what I had been put on Earth for.

Mostly I mothered the way I knew. I used instinct. I didn't examine or reflect much. Loving my baby felt like enough. I bumbled through each day somehow. It was my life, and it felt good. We laughed a lot. My son was a little slow with his milestones, so of course I worried about that. He was also very cute, very funny, and—the new mother's blessing—he was a good sleeper. I was fortunate to have family nearby and a group of friends who were also new moms. We supported each other, which normalized our daily lives and kept me going. We muddled through similar new-mom experiences and went to the same wonderful nurse at the local baby health center—she set us straight when necessary and mostly gave us confidence.

Of course there was also tedium and loneliness. My husband traveled a lot, taking his first overseas trip when our baby was a week old. I didn't flinch; I managed. It was the way of the world then, and I didn't question what was essentially family and cultural tradition. I was with my baby nearly every minute of the day, and my job was to look after him and our home while my husband worked. Combined with this was a stubbornness and a desire, especially in the early days, to do it by myself. I wanted to do it my way without advice and with little help. This was my gig.

While I thought I could do it all, sometimes there was no adult in charge in the room.

Sometimes I was emotionally absent. I didn't give myself permission to take a break or to look after myself. I didn't think I deserved it. When I look back now, I know that had I taken some time out to fulfill myself, I could have nourished my baby boy more. The saying that advises mothers to put the oxygen mask on themselves first wasn't in vogue yet.

Many moments of my first-time mothering were rigid. My whole being was wrapped up in my baby and in trying to conform as much as I could to the social ideals of mothering and doing it properly, "by the book." Feelings of ambivalence were a no-no. Penelope Leach's book *Your Baby & Child*[76] was my bible at the time, and I don't recall any references to feelings of ambivalence, or if there were I must have conveniently skipped over them. The notion of owning conflicting feelings about mothering and naming my resentments, loneliness, anger, and despair did not exist for me. I conflated any feelings of ambivalence with being a "bad" mom. I had no understanding of the idea of ambivalence or its value.

I was also struggling with my identity. I had always wanted to work and found so much gratification in it, but I couldn't figure out how to combine it with mothering. It was too difficult to go out and leave my baby. I wrestled with constant feelings of guilt, and whenever I was away I couldn't wait to get back to him. I was stuck. I decided to compromise and return to tutoring from home. However good my intentions were, though, I sabotaged myself. I was unable to find a separate space for myself and my work, so I worked from home with a toddler running around most of the time. I didn't realize that I needed help from someone external who could offer clarity and guidance. Of course, in hindsight, it could have been much simpler. If I had set myself up properly with a stronger support system, and also trusted my love for my child and myself equally, I could have continued to tutor, which I loved to do, and to be a mom. I was all-consumed by the need to live up to the maternal ideal, to be that perfect mom, and looking back I wish I had been able to let the other side of myself flourish. At the time, I was too rigid and lacked the insight to understand that I could do both.

My somewhat meandering path toward having another child came with an experience of secondary infertility, an inability to have a second child, which I can only describe as a personal tsunami. Until then, I never really questioned the course of my life. I was in for a shock. I was about twenty-six, and it upended me totally and rocked my beliefs about myself and my world. I was in total denial, and I clearly remember thinking, "This happens to other people, not to me." I spun totally out of control. I was hit with a deep pain and yearning and found myself suddenly questioning my whole being. The battle against infertility took over my life. Treatment cycles brought a roller coaster of elation and disappointment, multiple early miscarriages, and days of sadness and hopelessness, loneliness and heartache. I lost my purpose and my confidence. Then I began questioning my beliefs and my identity as my world became uprooted. I was in total despair and seemingly cut off from the world, just walking like a robot, one foot in front of the other.

Fertility treatment in the early '80s was both cutting edge and fledgling. There was taboo and shame connected with it for me and little knowledge about the need for emotional support. I found it soul-destroying. My self-confidence was already at an all-time low, and the clinics reinforced this. You were a number and were treated as such; there was very little humanity. I already felt so ashamed about not being able to conceive and to give my child a sibling. The dreams of a life that I had mapped out for myself, with the three or four children and the happy home, was in shambles. I recognized that I was a shell of my former self, but I was unable to talk to anyone about my life or my infertility, and I didn't seek professional help. My treatment was a secret and so was my life. I was totally guarded and frightened about everything. My major fear was that I wouldn't have another child and what that would mean for me. How could I keep going? I felt that if I showed my true despair to my husband, I would be fighting a battle on another front. He didn't understand my feelings of failure and emptiness, my yearnings. I was scared that he would try to get me to stop the treatments, not understanding that this was the only thing that was keeping me going. Cycle after cycle, I was absolutely driven—hope then disappointment, hope then more disappointment. It became my life's mission. My whole personality changed. I was truly sad, and I would say now that I was suffering from depression, but I didn't know who or what to turn to. I was gagged. I couldn't speak. All I knew was that if I didn't succeed with having another child, then I didn't know how I would get through my life. I felt completely powerless.

This persisted over the next six years. My world revolved around my infertile identity. But I was strong; I kept going.

I felt pessimistic, but there was no choice except to keep trying. Then, in a miraculous turn of events, I became pregnant naturally while I was taking a two-month break from treatment. It seemed like an impossible coincidence, though now I understand it on a physical and emotional level. The reset for my body allowed an opportunity for my mind to also recalibrate and rest. In this break from treatment, I registered that there was no chance for conception, so I completely surrendered control. And my body took over naturally. I clearly remember a peacefulness, and for the first time in many years, I even cuddled a friend's baby. I willingly let my guard down and can recall the warm feeling spreading over my body when I held her baby.

While some medics may doubt or deny that there are biological and emotional links to fertility, my story of my own psychological block disputes this. While there was a physical basis to my infertility, there was also an emotional component. This was my time.

It is hard to put words to the magnitude of feelings that this pregnancy brought. It was life-changing. There was total elation, triumph, and disbelief. The pregnancy itself was both wonderful and fraught. I insisted on having continual ultrasounds for reassurance, I bonded quickly, and maybe foolishly, with this baby, and at about week twenty-six, I had a bleed. The moment of crisis fortunately passed, and there were other scares, but it was still a joyous time. I was so grateful.

This pregnancy healed a deep internal wound for me. The birth of my second son was a recovery, a restitution—setting things right. I was back on track and blessed once again with an easy infant who was cute and wonderful. I think maybe both my children matched with a naïve baby part of myself at this time of my life. I was totally fulfilled, and my needs were answered. This was a blissful time. I felt that I had my complete family. And I felt whole. Of course, there were daily struggles and interruptions, but I felt that the sun was shining for me.

Similarly, during my second experience as a new mom, I closed my eyes to my feelings of ambivalence. Seven years of secondary infertility meant I felt so blessed and grateful that I didn't allow any other feelings to penetrate.

Then my next maternal challenge occurred. Another unexpected plot twist, as my husband and I separated, and I faced mothering alone. When I ponder this experience, though very difficult, it equally forced me to learn to stand on my own two feet as I protected and loved my boys. I knew I would be okay. There is no doubt that my whole family was rocked to its core, and both of my children experienced pain. While I tried to be as emotionally present as I could, I was indeed absent at times.

When I look back on these times, though, I recognize there is a deep divide in the way I managed the crises of infertility and solo mothering. When infertility descended on me, I couldn't surrender to it. It made me question my being and pushed me further into rigidity, so that I was dreading my future. I was threatened. Solo mothering presented a different darkness for me. It was a different kind of loss. I had to keep moving; I had to survive the uncertainty. I was responsible for my children. I couldn't remain stuck or petrified, frozen in a pattern that served only myself. I leaned into the messiness and the uncertainty and reached out for help. I used therapy to rework my inner world. I learned that

I needed to be the adult, although often I wasn't, that life is uncertain, and that I would pull through somehow. I tried my best to protect my children, although sometimes I failed, and I learned to surrender to my situation and just sit with it. While my infertility experience took loneliness to a new level, where I was cut off and despairing, in solo mothering I depended on my therapy and exposing my vulnerability until I became independent. At the depths of this darkness, a wise friend told me that one day I would understand. I didn't know what she was saying at the time, and now I do. I needed to go solo to prepare myself for my future. It seems to me that the universe conspired and gave me another chance to mother—this time, myself—to re-establish my sense of self in a new, healthier way.

The main theme that was running through these stages of my mothering was my initial incapacity to face and process my range of feelings, my ambivalence. At the time I began my solo mothering, I could see that I had many issues to contend with, both external and internal. By finding a gifted therapist, I was able to summon the courage and realize the necessity of working with and surrendering to my feelings.

At age thirty-nine, my solo parenting came to an end, and with this came a chance to reunite with my husband. This was followed at forty by a surprise pregnancy that set off a time of reflection and surrendering. I was in total shock after the years of infertility and aware of feelings of both excitement and trepidation. I was concerned about the possible health complications for myself and the baby, and I had two healthy children. Why tempt fate? What would my new life look like with a newborn, an eight-year-old, and a seventeen-year-old? I embarked on a conscious thought process, something that was never part of my previous pregnancies. It forced me to gather together all my feelings, my fears, my delights, my anticipations, my guilt, and my ambivalence, which I had to accept and try to understand. Despite the turmoil, I knew in my heart that this baby was meant to be, that we would be okay, and that I would face the new challenges with a full heart. Hope and the future took over for me. I was once again in the thrall of pregnancy. The thought of returning to nappies, a newborn, and sleepless nights did not concern me; I was overjoyed.

With this birth, I loved the return to my hands-on mothering. I appreciated every opportunity and experience: the soft skin and the folds at the back of my baby's neck, the bliss, the afterglow of the feeding. While at forty-one I was a little more tired physically, I totally surrendered to it. This baby girl taught me so much. From the beginning, it was clear to me that this baby was not passive and that I was going to be directed by her much of the time—another new and entirely different mothering experience, which was much more fluid. I had fun with it, and it seemed sometimes like I was quasi-grandparenting. My baby and I found a fit. When I was rigid, it just didn't work, and I recognized this and took it in stride. Most of our clashes occurred when I didn't surrender to the chaos and allow for imperfection. I could now engage with my feelings about my mothering with reflection, truth, and freedom. When I was forty-six, I returned to part-time work as a psychotherapist.

When I look back at how my mothering unfolded, I can't help thinking that while it was a bumpy ride, a roller coaster of ups and downs, this was how I needed to learn and become my strongest self as a person and mother, and it's only through life experience that this happens.

There were still a few surprises in store for me in the mothering arena and a lot of lessons for me that came out of left field. When I reached the age of about fifty, I noticed a change. I'd been hands-on mothering for twenty-seven years, and that realization coincided with menopause. I wanted my own life, and I felt resentment. My daughter had to shoulder most of this because she was the youngest and the only child left at home. This was a new challenge to navigate, and though we had our moments, she was able to convey her displeasure with me, and I was eventually able to meet her feelings with flow rather than resistance. And anyway, unlike the way that I was brought up, any rigidity at this point didn't feel right. I received the gift of a child who was honest, strong, and unconventional, who was able to say it as it was and continually challenged me about the way I lived my life. This caused me to think deeply about my mothering, past and present, and to consider how I could do things differently.

This final mothering experience allowed me to gather together what I had learned from my previous years, to discover my voice, and to meet with and learn from my ambivalent feelings. I began to reflect on my range of feelings and to lean into them, to really question the way I mothered, and to try to understand its dynamic. My earlier mothering and wider life experiences had somewhat prepared me to be more confident, to be able to listen more carefully, to more readily accept criticism, and to judge myself and others less. I also began to understand and work with my body signals. I recognized that fatigue was a sign that I wasn't coping and that maybe I needed some time out. I learned to be aware of how I reacted to my weariness and how to be present. I shut out many social expectations that I realized didn't matter and were damaging. I could see that the ideals and expectations that I had relied on in my earlier mothering were just not going to hold water this time. Maintaining the relationship with my child blocked out a lot of the outside noise. It was paramount.

I knew that my child could teach me as long as I remained open to learning. When my daughter turned fourteen, I understood that I would need to be present during her last years of school. This time, I was fluid in my thinking, and I took the opportunity to both be available to my youngest child and to accomplish a long-desired dream of writing my PhD. We bonded over schoolwork together. It was no accident that I would research mothering.

Around this time, my brother got divorced, and another change to our family life was dawning. My two nephews essentially became part of our nuclear family. While they didn't live with us, they spent a lot of time in our home. They had totally free and welcome access. My youngest and her cousins gave me another opportunity to mother. The house was full of fun and laughter, vitality and warmth. Their hilarious antics took the notion of flow to new levels, and I adjusted my expectations accordingly. Ironically, as I became older, I was able to embrace fun much more easily and truthfully. Maybe as a young mother I found it hard to have fun and be fluid because I thought I had to know it all and be grown up, when I was, in reality, still a child. My sense of play emerged as I grew into my mothering. My deep belly laughs took me by surprise, and I was often the fourth cog in the wheel of their fun.

When I look back at my mothering, I often wonder what kept me going, showing up every day to do the best I could. It's so difficult to try something new, to lean into the uncertainty, and to go down an unorthodox road. It's scary to contemplate change, which fills you with self-doubt, but when we surrender to the curve balls in life, they often come back in unexpected ways.

Now in my sixties, as the mother of adult children, I'm mostly comfortable with my mothering, and I am able to admit to and value my ambivalent feelings. It's taken a lot of work to arrive here—lots of courage, pain, and honest reflection. I still wrestle every day to let go of my guilt and to stop myself from judging my adult children. I realize that self-forgiveness and flexibility is crucial. I am mindful that my exchanges with my children are as transparent as possible, rather than colored by my expectations. My adult children are able to make their own life choices, some sound and others perhaps not so, but this is their life. I now know that is their struggle, and when things are difficult for them, it is not my job to fix it, even if I could. I have learned to listen, to not interfere, to hold my tongue, and to be interested and curious. I am beyond proud of my adult children and the paths they have chosen.

As my children have become adults, I have found new ways to steady myself and to rely on my thinking space to monitor and guard against thoughtless reactions. I try to be as patient and present as I can, and I have learned the value of the "pause." By readily engaging with my wide range of feelings, I muster my tenderness and compassion more easily.

I seek clarity in my choices and constantly strive to get the balance right. I credit the work that I have done on ambivalence and the worth that it places on all feelings; the inclusive *and* rather than the excluding force of *or* is a guiding force for me. This mantra accompanies me every moment of every day in all my mothering and wider experiences.

By writing openly about this subject, I have of course opened myself and my mothering to plenty of outside judgment. Margo is writing about that, so what does that mean about how she feels about her children? What person in their right mind goes down this path? Sometimes I think it would have been easier to sit under a tree and watch the world pass by. Scrutinizing the tropes and beliefs attached to mothering revealed something about myself to me, my struggles and joys. And equally, I have received so much back: an ongoing quest to understand myself and my mothering; the privilege of supporting other mothers as I take care to normalize their experiences and not to judge them; the joy of knowing that I have helped to validate even only one young mom, to help her in her daily life to feel that she's understood, that her feelings are normal, and much more to the point, that these feelings are valuable and must be heard and claimed.

The gap between the maternal ideal and reality needs to be named and claimed so we can disentangle unreachable expectations from actual everyday mothering. I keep returning to my premise that along with its joys and pleasures, many parts of mothering are messy, often unfulfilling, tiring, frustrating. A mother's pain and suffering is aggravated by the subconscious message that a mother should always love unconditionally. Maternal loneliness and attempting to keep up with the ideal are constant companions for many mothers. We need to find creative ways to deal with our feelings as fully as we can. Our greatest lessons often come as we mother on the edge. Experiences of disruption and pain make us stronger and more resilient and allow us to develop more understanding. Despite these immense challenges, we emerge in a robust space, and when we discover our voice, we empower ourselves and free ourselves from the ideal.

As mothers, we learn "on the job" from our life's best teachers: our children. They shine a light on our flaws, and if we are prepared to pay attention to them, we can learn from our mistakes, the source of our wisdom. The "smarts" in life are not always connected to formal education, degrees, and the like. On the contrary, academic theory and a total reliance on books can often block deep emotional change and real inner knowledge.

Over the years, I have learned to embrace and live with the conflicts and contradictions inherent in mothering. My voice has evolved such that I am more compassionate with myself and my children. Through my own evolution, professional and personal, I can recognize and give credence to the struggles that have accompanied each stage, to see them in context, and rather than admonish myself as before, I admit to and reconcile my feelings of guilt and shame. I went into each new mothering experience with vigor, and while I emerged with some emotional bruising, I still survived.

Writing this book has allowed me to get a firmer grip on what maternal ambivalence really means and why it needs to be securely fastened to the language of mothering. The first step has been to demystify and explain the particular type of ambivalence that belongs to mothers as clearly as possible. This involves our admission that wider society, including us as mothers, has colluded with false stories and narratives about mothering. In a sense, we have betrayed motherhood. When we can remove the myths and stigma that surround mothering, then we can earn the courage to voice and own all our feelings.

Applying ambivalence to mothering adds another layer. While the definition makes sense in most relationships and workings, once it is used in mothering, taboo and silence must be acknowledged. As Barbara Almond reminds us, whereas having hating feelings toward anyone but one's child is tolerable, for a mother it is considered "immoral, unnatural, and evil."[77] This distinction lies at the heart of society's hypocrisy when it comes to mothering and the refusal to entertain ideas suggestive of ambivalence. But it has led me to think about the wider convictions guiding my life that are embedded in this word. So much of what I believe in and how I live my life, personally and professionally, is connected with the notion of ambivalence, where contradictory emotions exist together. There is always more than one side to any situation. Flow is crucial, and rigidity is deadening. Letting go of judgment and expectations is imperative, and there is immense value in struggle and confrontation. In fact, ambivalence has become a major determinant in my life.

Mothering is not what any of us imagine. Surprising and shocking experiences occur that take us beyond what we may have anticipated, as we are continually thrown into the unknown and try different ways to keep afloat, particularly in distressing situations. Both unexpected and everyday incidents have led me to reflect and learn as I try to integrate both my own and others' past experiences into my current non-hands-on mothering. There are so many complicated feelings that assault our mothering—shame, blame, doubt, and guilt. It is only when we accept this reality that we allow ourselves the opportunity to mother more humanely. By engaging with all our feelings, we can embrace the truth that mothering is bittersweet—that even in its dark moments, we can find some light. As mothers, it is our job to capture the sunny moments and to struggle with the darker ones, and to refuse to allow the bleak times to paralyze and defeat the joyous times. Struggling with the dark moments takes us to the light.

EIGHT

WHAT KEEPS US GOING?

LET'S STOP FOR A MOMENT, regroup, and make sure we are on the same page. Maternal ambivalence is a mother's inner, dynamic practice of owning and holding together all her maternal feelings, many of which are contradictory, without throwing away the uncomfortable ones, those that confront and unsettle her. These disturbing feelings are nestled in what I call her motherlove, the feelings that keep her upright as they cushion her from the ravages of her everyday mothering. Her maternal feelings—including enjoyment, delight, resentment, anger, doubt, fear, misgivings, recriminations, grievances, even hating feelings—conflict, collide, and move every which way, and the chances are that most of us haven't yet put a name to this sensation. While we are familiar with it, we aren't sure how, or even whether, to talk about it, what to do with it, or where it belongs. This is maternal ambivalence.

It's so important for all of us as mothers to own our ambivalence, to acknowledge the push and pull of mothering—the bittersweet. To value and to gather all our feelings, both dark and light, and to give them a voice. To take responsibility for our own truths and our personal stories. This isn't so straightforward, because it means that we must give ourselves permission to experience our unspeakable feelings, to admit that they belong to us and, further, that we have a right to them. We need to believe that all our feelings are normal, despite the anxiety that exists around the monstrous ones, and that they live in the context of our ever-sustaining love and have value. This runs counter to our beliefs; it's a disruption. I turn the traditional beliefs about mothering upside down by shining a curious and nonjudgmental light on the underbelly, and mostly hidden side, of mothering rather than rejecting it and focusing on its more acceptable face. Looking at all the sides, including the distasteful, dirty, messy experiences, ironically empowers the mother and gives her agency as it consolidates the truth of her experience rather than questioning it.

As I continue to observe mothering and to write about it, I wonder what keeps us going and what makes it a positive and transformative process. My last book[78] concluded with some personal, regretful musings I had about my hands-on mothering: If only I had slowed down, been less serious, and laughed more. If only I'd played longer at bath time, been willing for my children to be late to school a few times, insisted on fewer after-school activities, and allowed myself more "me" time.

In writing this book, I found myself holding onto and yet recasting these misgivings into a more forward-looking perspective focused on what I know now, which is the certainty that as mothers, we can make change within ourselves and spur other mothers to do the same; that we can identify and think about our experiences, name our feelings, and remain fluid in our outlook; that we can do less second-guessing and judging about ourselves and our children in the face of social etiquette.

There are plenty of practical, concrete ways to begin owning our feelings rather than allowing them to control us, to appreciate the value of showing up every day in the best possible way we can, and to see the merit in continually repairing our mistakes and trying to limit our expectations. It sounds so straightforward, but of course it's not simple to achieve these lofty ambitions overnight or to disentangle from the emotional maelstrom that is mothering. Mistakes will always be made—you wouldn't be a mother if they weren't.

The tools and strategies I've outlined in this chapter will hopefully help to guide and give you the opportunity to think more about your mothering. They come as both gentle and not-so-gentle reminders; they are signposts to guide us. Consider this an interactive experience—make it a literal checklist of goals and priorities, find what works for you, and leave some room for the unexpected feelings and interruptions in the everyday.

- **Claim your individual approach to mothering.** Celebrate its uniqueness and find your own words to name your experience. This may prompt you to think about it in a new way, to open your mindset, and to rethink the ones that you may have been holding onto for all your life—possibly since you were a child yourself.

- **Don't go it alone.** A mother needs a village, both emotional and physical, to raise herself and her child, so find your team. Surround yourself with energy givers, not takers. Support can come from a partner, who can share the load and the joy, as well as other moms, chosen friends, and family. Learn to discriminate between those who are givers and those who are takers, and stick with those who encourage you, those who fill you up rather than deplete you, and those whom you can depend on and trust.

o **Making mistakes and fixing them is mothering.** Acknowledge your failures for what they are. A mother needs to understand that one of the most crucial parts of mothering revolves around the continual and shifting process of making mistakes and repairing them. Know that they will happen again. And most importantly, learn from them.

o **Give yourself credit.** And a pat on the back when you get something right. When you have some sort of triumph, no matter how small, acknowledge it. Remember that getting it right even once out of three or four times means movement in the right direction. Muscle memory is developed over time, not overnight.

o **Name your feelings.** Learn to recognize them and their symptoms. Often there is a bodily sensation that goes with them, perhaps a racing heart when you feel doubt or pity or sweaty palms when you get nervous. Rather than judging yourself, recognize what your feelings mean. Confront what is scary and holds a stigma for you, engaging with it rather than repressing it. In time, and in naming it, its power fades.

○ **Maintain a sense of flow.** Put this idea into practice by entering into your taboo areas as often as the opportunity presents itself. Discover your own underbelly and claim your fed-up, ugly side. In doing this, we embrace and learn from uncomfortable, self-loathing feelings and accept ourselves with honesty. Only when we can do this can we develop a strong core— and become stronger, more loving mothers to our children. Make fluid sensations such as hope, forgiveness, compassion, surrendering, and gratitude a familiar and consistent part of your mothering.

○ **Recognize the difference between response and reaction.** A response is a measured reply to an action. It means that you have given yourself space as you allow your feelings to wash over you, and the time to reflect rather than act. If necessary, take ten deep breaths. A knee-jerk reaction without thought so often leaves a mother unhappy and guilty with how she acted toward her child. You learn to understand and be aware of your reactions, what triggers you. Recognize them and write them down, if helpful. For example, what do you do when it gets to be too much? Go to bed? Call your mom? Lock yourself in your room? Hand your child over to someone to shield yourself and him from your pain? Scream at your partner? Can you do it better, differently, for them and for yourself in particular?

○ **Honor the melting moments.** Those times when our hearts soften to jelly in an exchange with our child. These feelings of overwhelming love, often mixed with pity, desire, and longing, are often a recognition of some type of maternal loss. Find meaning in your melting moments; they are usually reminders of something deeper. They can renew and recharge our love, a gratifying reminder that we are alive and able to engage in our rawest feelings.

○ **Give yourself some time out.** When you give yourself what you need, whether it's a hobby, exercise, professional work, or just quiet time for yourself, you can be more present for your children.

○ **Laugh as much as possible.** If there is a humorous side to any situation, find it and take things less seriously.

○ **Be accountable for your feelings and actions.** This is a responsibility, not a choice, and by accepting this, we empower ourselves as mothers. We need to own and claim the feelings that belong to us, and to use language that suits us without judging others or ourselves for our words. This is our job as much as mothering is. It is the achievement that marks our agency.

○ **Beware of rigidity.** Perfection is rigid. It is a myth that we cannot live up to, yet on some level still hope for. Mothers don't always fall in love with their baby at first sight. Mothers aren't ever-giving and fully present all the time. Myths such as these are damaging and untrue and set us up for failure from the beginning. They also undermine the beautiful truth that mothering is an experience of continual failure and repair in which recovery and renewal exist. This is the reality of mothering. Perfection is a fairy tale to keep us in a fantasyland. In simple words: lower the bar.

○ **Be aware of the gap between ideals and reality.** Develop an awareness of the limits of ideals and how they play out for you as a mother, how they interfere with your mothering, what their purpose is, and where and how to tackle them. Mothering means embracing daily contradictions and seeing them in real terms rather than as expectations that cannot be met, even though that's what we might like them to be or be used to doing.

○ **Take care not to slide into indifference.** Avoid cutting off emotionally from your child. Though it might be seductive to sever and retreat to your cocoon in the tough moments, it stifles and minimizes you and your child. Its effects can't be repaired and cannot be learned from or transformed. Rather than succumbing to rigidity and expectations, remain in the fight and the struggle. Indifference is a slippery and irredeemable slope.

○ **Let go of certainty and the pretense that it exists.** The truth is, the only control we have is the realization that we really have no control. This can be an empowering insight. Lean into uncertainty and embrace the notion of getting lost and finding your way, that things will work out in the long run, despite the fact that it most likely won't be in the way you expect. Embracing uncertainty can open us up to curiosity and creativity, open us to change. Certainty belongs to the myth of ideals and does not exist.

○ **Limit words that prompt rigidity such as shame, blame, and should.** We need to use words that represent what feels right in mothering; the tone of our language is crucial.

○ **Limit social media influence.** Modern technology has many benefits and drawbacks. Some tips for us as moms, especially those of us in early years when we end up spending a lot of time on our phones:

  ▪ Reminder #1: Recognize the risks and benefits that social media presents today. Be aware of how much our lives are magnified, and often almost distorted, by it because we are so intimately exposed to, and a part of, the virtual world. Social media presents a biased view of life, only some of which may be real, and much of it is often a creation. There is a slant that others want to show on social media platforms.

  ▪ Reminder #2: Make a commitment to yourself to limit social media, especially when you are hands-on mothering. I am not suggesting that you abandon your phone; it's not all-or-nothing. My tip is to cut down in a way that is manageable for you.

  ▪ Reminder #3: Social media does have its benefits. It spreads information and brings people together.

- ○ **Find your mantras.** Mine include, "All mothers do their best," and, "We are all making it up as we go along." Or, to borrow Joh's words, we "muddle through," and all of us are just "looking to pick up their pieces, however they have been scattered." We can glean a lot from these ideas.

- ○ **Be real about what mothering is to you.** While it may be a messy, interrupted experience, at the same time, we need to remind ourselves that it is also the most exhilarating and gratifying experience. As Emma Heaphy (@wordsof_emmaheaphy) wisely remarks on her Instagram post from April 25, 2022, "It's no wonder we are made and broken simultaneously some days."[79] Go figure.

We have choice. We can rewrite our own story. It can be a narrative that replies to the question, "Am I a terrible mother?" with a truthful answer, a fluid one that goes something like this: "Sometimes I am, and sometimes I'm not." It's an answer that relies on *and* rather than *or*, that befriends ambivalence and leans into our scary and uncomfortable feelings. Motherhood isn't a happily-ever-after fairy tale in the traditional sense; it's a teapot with many battle scars and china chinks, but that's where its beauty and humanity really lies. Mothering is not an easy experience, or one that can be done in a meaningful way by rote or without getting our hands dirty. We must give ourselves some slack.

I remind myself almost daily about my niece's words and her powerful message about maternal ambivalence as she sees it: her realization that it is so much a part of her daily interactions with her children, that it has empowered her because she can now give her feelings a name; and her compassionate appeal that it's our right to name our feelings, that the words we use are ours and we must own them. The vulnerability and strength in Joh's words as she normalizes and questions the ideal of what a mother is meant to put up with is bolstered by her thoughtfulness about the type of help she would accept and from whom. She was able to absorb lessons—that is, value—from her difficult experiences, such as resilience as she relied on her convictions while signaling the fragility of postnatal health. I am inspired by Joh's bravery as she battles with uncertainty and somehow maintains hope. Her piercing words speak the truth and help to inform my language.

An understanding of mothering, its pushes and pulls, its messiness, is critical: a mothering that relies on acceptance and surrendering, the reframing of a rigid ideal to a functioning and shifting narrative—this is maternal ambivalence as a fruitful, central, and valuable part of daily mothering.

The idea of maternal ambivalence disrupts and reimagines mothering. It is a positive dynamic that we don't readily talk about, a large part of our experience as mothers. We need to welcome the entirety of each day and the reality that our feelings occur on a spectrum: the feelings of joy, contentment, and happiness together with the distress, fatigue, boredom, resentment, panic, anger, blame, guilt, shame, and even hating flashes. By claiming and welcoming all our feelings, we can have a richer and more honest relationship with ourselves and our children. This legitimizes and gives all our feelings, the loving ones and the dark ones, a voice.

NINE

REACHING
MATERNAL WISDOM

THE LENS OF AMBIVALENCE GIVES us an opportunity to think more truthfully and imaginatively about our mothering and to revolutionize the maternal conversation. As the term "maternal ambivalence" becomes more familiar, the complexities and troubling aspects of mothering become more recognizable and acceptable. While it goes against our grain as mothers and wider social ideals for us to value our murky parts, they help us to find our voice. By owning and being curious about our full maternal feelings, by surrendering to them, we can identify and own our own version of ambivalence. This is an accomplishment. This is the essence of maternal ambivalence.

How do I want to conclude this book? What do I want to leave you with? Some words of wisdom, which are embedded in our ambivalence. Words that can help us to pick ourselves up when we stumble as mothers.

I have a monthly discussion with three women who work with me on my social media outreach. The founder and owner of the company, who is the new mom to a six-month-old and a toddler; a younger woman who crafts the posts and who has no children; and a close colleague of mine from Sydney, who has six children aged six to eighteen—they all share my passion and belief in maternal ambivalence and my insistence that it is an unsung, central, and invaluable part of mothering.

Up to a few weeks ago, our meetings were for the most part purely business. Last month, I asked this question of the new mom: "Are you welcoming your ambivalence?" This query prompted a resounding "yes" from her and set off a deluge of responses and thinking from the team. The new mom followed this up with stories of how her newfound acquaintance with this idea of ambivalence has encouraged her to examine, name, and work through her feelings. Being able to express and own her raw sensitivities helps to calm her fears and to make "sense of the confusion" and the multiple overwhelming emotions that often occur all at once in her mothering. Accepting that mothering necessarily brings a range of feelings that are often contradictory has allowed her to be increasingly comfortable with her daily life and to recognize that she is "doing okay." She adds that this is all "very real." What a leveler for me!

The new mom then recounted a current concern, her second thoughts about leaving her children with her husband for a few days so she could have time away with her girlfriends. She describes the conflicting emotions of this lived experience. She realizes that she will desperately miss her babies, but at the same time, she needs some time away, a few carefree days and a chance to be "fed" by her friends. After years of COVID and pregnancy, she knows that if she doesn't take the opportunity now, she never will. Her husband totally supports her and plans to take the week off work to be with his little daughters. She even survives her own mother's petition not to go: "How can you leave them with their father? He's the one that needs the break." An echo of the maternal ideal, the inconsistent expectations about men and women, and the possible underlying message that questions whether she is a fit mother. Rather than being held back by rigidity and rules, she decides to seize the opportunity for a break—to go with the flow.

I am struck with the realization that many women really do understand what I am getting at. This bolsters me to encourage mothers to talk about their feelings of ambivalence and to make a space to recognize their value. The new mom describes how a soap commercial on television in which a few older moms gather and muse over their earlier mothering experiences continues to affect her. These mothers talk about the regrets they feel because they are no longer holding their babies, wishing that they could still be in that phase of life. This reminds me of that saying about rearing children, that the days are long and the years are short. She adds that even thinking about this commercial makes her teary, and it has become a routine for her to watch it at the beginning of every week as a prompt for her to slow down and treasure these times when her daughters are young. During the conversation, she pays me a memorable compliment. She refers to working with us at this time in her mothering as a "crazy advantage." This new mom is telling me that my work helps her to be vulnerable to the silenced and dark feelings of her mothering, that it gives her a space to think, to feel held, and to be emotionally fed by its messaging. How random is this but also how honest and wise?

The youngest woman of the group spoke about how she now recognizes that ambivalence comes up in many other places, in her own life and in business. What really seems to strike her is how some of the problems of new mothers and young business entrepreneurs coincide. She recounts her discussions with some entrepreneurs and their complaints about the difficulties that they encounter, often craving their old unencumbered life with its freedom and simplicity. While the similarity of these words and feelings resonated with her, her understanding of ambivalence—of the value of sitting with contradictory feelings rather than looking for an escape route—allowed her to clearly see the difference between life as a mother and life as an entrepreneur. For the mother, sending her baby back is simply not an option. She must find a way to push through, to manage, and to somehow reconcile her difficulties as part and parcel of her mothering, to learn from them and to somehow use her pain and struggle to nourish her love for her child. This young woman could now appreciate that the entrepreneurs could learn a lot from this approach, to take on rather than to relinquish challenges by changing jobs or trying to go back to the old life, to adopt the mothers' approach: when the going gets tough, the tough get going. She really embraced the idea that ambivalence, a crucial part of our everyday interactions and relationships, needs to be more widely understood.

Then my colleague of many years, who has older children, introduced another layer into the conversation by asking a question about what takes us away from being in the flow of our mothering and what pulls us in. She revealed the difficulties that she has of being present for all her children, who compete for her attention and often at the same time. And as a result, her children often air their grievances about it to her, leaving her feeling guilty and at a loss for what to do with her distressing emotions. As moms, we know exactly what she is saying. But how do we stay adult and work through these accusations? The temptation is to use power over one's child, to put an end to the scuffle, all the time knowing that power is never a good currency to use; it's not an answer. So much energy is needed to stay with the complaints, and the reality is that they hold both some truth *and* some fiction. It's not *or*, it's *both*. My colleague talks of the time constraints that she continues to feel, particularly with her large family, and the repetitive and relentless nature of daily life and how it often compromises her own needs. She bravely admits that mothering has never been quite enough for her and that she needs other challenges, something for herself. Trying to balance all this with the deep love she has for her children is the perennial struggle—the value of being able to meet our ambivalence.

It is not lost on me how closely I identify with all these experiences. They touch on the many layers of mothering, both contemporary and historical, and the ambivalence, the push and pull that as mothers we constantly feel in our daily life. The new mom knows that even though her own mother's version doesn't sit right with her, that it's still there—it's part of her story. Don't we all still listen to these deeply embedded voices? And there's the struggle that we all have as moms as we try to develop a thinking space despite the multiple interruptions. How do we manage our distress when our children dump on us? Our agony when our children know so well which buttons to press? Our worry about taking time out, both wanting and not wanting to have time apart from our children? Our guilt over putting our own needs first or even considering them? The continual struggle of getting it right?

And then there's the big issue with adult children: How do we let go properly? How do we get the tension of this tricky part of mothering right? It's probably just another stumble. We know that it will be conflictual and confronting; it won't be smooth. However, our difficult dark moments eventually send us back to the love we have for our children.

The words of these moms apply to me and most other moms I know. There's no stage when we don't mother. When we are hands-on, it's tough. When we are hands-off, it's tough. When we are 24/7, it's tough. When we separate, it's tough. Understanding the value of ambivalence is life-changing. In our stumbles, we learn, we get back up, we try to lean in. We flow. We each do it in our own way.

What I am getting at is that we can only reach wisdom through our lived experiences, by repairing them, adapting to them, and learning from them.

In his poem "On Children," Khalil Gibran[80] made some wise observations that have won the test of time. They are confronting in their truth, and they can help us as we let go of our children. He advises us against having expectations about our children: "But seek not to make them like you." He talks about bending and movement, and how as mothers it's our task to be stable and happy for our children in their tomorrow, which we cannot visit "even in our dreams." This is a compass for our mothering, a wake-up call, a reminder that our children's lives belong to them, not to us, and there are parts of their lives that we are not privy to. This is the raw truth of mothering, its essence. Our job is to send them off in the best and most secure way that we can.

A wise mother develops a deep emotional understanding of her child by learning from her own experiences, both joyful and difficult, which help her to connect the dots. She reaches a working and affective understanding of herself. She sees her causes and effects more clearly. She realizes that she can do the best for her child when she is in a place where she is okay with herself, when she can integrate her feelings.

She develops a maternal sixth sense, which activates before she reacts to her child: "When I do this, this might happen." It creates an inner connection.

She finds worth and meaning in the paradox, contradiction, chaos, and conflict that is mothering, even in the darkest hours, and acknowledges her own complicity in what goes wrong in her relationship with her child as she attempts to repair and resolve. She is able to learn from her mistakes. She is fluid, and she leans into her experiences. She surrenders to her mothering.

The wise mother continually asks herself why she colludes with strict maternal ideals and taboo, both her own and those that belong to society, whether they are too rigid or self-serving, whether they allow her to learn from experience. When we lean into the questions, often a scary and counterintuitive experience, we can get to untapped, valuable new places. We adapt to them rather than live by them. We recognize that our loyalty to ideals and their inflexibility hamper our truth as mothers and individuals.

A wise mother can tolerate and explore her troubling feelings toward her child. She can accommodate her distressing feelings and recognize them as part of her love rather than demonizing or judging them. She can remove the sting from moments of hate and see them as the means to sit with all of her feelings rather than closing a door to the abhorrent ones.

I'll share another lesson I've learned. A colleague who is well versed in mothering suggested to me that a wise mother does the right job for her children when she can first do the right job for herself. It sounds right of course, but it left me with a lot of unanswered questions: What does the "right job" mean? How do we measure this? My mind wandered to that airline message about putting the oxygen mask on yourself first before helping your child and the possibility that it will offer a guide.

Mothering is a complicated maze with many mixed messages and inferences, and this saying bears this out. The first part of the message tells us that we each have our own masks. We are separate. However, this separation runs contrary to our emotional and social programming that demands that we are continually available to our child. The reality is that we both are and aren't separate. The next part of the message flips us back to a close involvement as we are told to help our child with his or her mask. Then that is overturned as we are soon faced with our child growing up, and we become dispensable much of the time. This is a reminder of something so essential to mothering: its contrariness and its confusion. We often find ourselves in an emotional whirlpool as we swing between wanting freedom from and holding tightly onto our child, the endless shifting between dependence and independence.

As moms, we are expected to move through these stages seamlessly, but usually we don't. We experience the push and pull of mothering. The ambivalence. How do we manage this and still hold onto and strengthen our love for our child? I believe the answer lies in being able to surrender to our mothering, accepting its expansions and contractions, avoiding the temptation to be rigid and to moralize, and just trying to get the balance right.

For me, this means holding on and learning as I stumble, claiming my voice and anchoring myself to a firm inner ground despite the continual storms brewing around me. It means paying attention to all the competing demands circling around me and working out which seems to be most pressing at any one moment, surrounding myself with others who support and understand me, those who fill me with energy as I free myself from those who drain me. It's finding a thinking place to keep me the grounded adult, to respect both my own and my child's needs, and remembering to be grateful. It's being aware of the importance of flow, which goes hand in hand with compassion and laughter.

All of this takes so much effort.

The idea that the mother needs to take symbolic "oxygen," to nourish herself in order to do the right job for herself and her child, is sound. It's the sign of a wise mother.

Maternal wisdom: it's not a state that you achieve but a work in progress.

ENDNOTES

1   Parker, Rozsika (2005). *Torn in Two: The Experience of Maternal Ambivalence* (Revised ed.). London, UK: Virago.

2   Parker, *Torn in Two*, p. 6.

3   Parker, *Torn in Two*, p. 6.

4   Solomon, Hester (2002). "Love: Paradox of Self and Other," in David Mann (ed.), *Love and Hate: Psychoanalytic Perspectives*. East Sussex, UK: Brunner-Routledge.

5   Solomon, "Love: Paradox of Self and Other," p. 56.

6   *Macquarie Dictionary*, https://www.macquariedictionary.com.au/.

7   Almond, Barbara (2010). *The Monster Within: The Hidden Side of Motherhood*. Oakland, CA: University of California Press.

8   Almond, *The Monster Within*, p. 2.

9   Parker, *Torn in Two*, p. 20.

10 Parker, *Torn in Two*, p. 6.

11 Mann, David (2002). "In Search of Love and Hate," in David Mann (ed.), *Love and Hate: Psychoanalytic Perspectives*. East Sussex, UK: Brunner-Routledge.

12 Mann, "In Search of Love and Hate," p. 45.

13 *Macquarie Dictionary*, https://www.macquariedictionary.com.au/.

14 Furman, Erna (2001). *On Being and Having a Mother*. Madison, CT: International Universities Press.

15 Furman, *On Being and Having a Mother*, p. 15.

16   Baraitser, Lisa (2009). *Maternal Encounters: The Ethics of Interruption*. London, UK: Taylor & Francis.

17   Baraitser, *Maternal Encounters*, p. 157.

18   Furman, *On Being and Having a Mother*, p. 15

19   Furman, *On Being and Having a Mother*, p. 40.

20   Furman, *On Being and Having a Mother*, p. 206.

21   Furman, *On Being and Having a Mother*, p. 39.

22   Furman, *On Being and Having a Mother*, p. 40.

23   *Lady Bird* (2017). Directed by Greta Gerwig [film]. United States: Universal Pictures.

24   Furman, *On Being and Having a Mother*, p. 70.

25   Furman, *On Being and Having a Mother*, p. 40.

26   Rye, Gill (2009). *Narratives of Mothering: Women's Writing in Contemporary France*. Newark, DE: University of Delaware Press.

27   Rye, *Narratives of Mothering*, p. 19.

28   Baraitser, *Maternal Encounters*, p. 67.

29   Baraitser, *Maternal Encounters*, p. 3.

30   Baraitser, *Maternal Encounters*, p. 4.

31   Baraitser, *Maternal Encounters*, p. 75.

32   Baraitser, *Maternal Encounters*, p. 73.

33   Baraitser, *Maternal Encounters*, p. 75.

34   Baraitser, *Maternal Encounters*, p. 87.

35   Baraitser, *Maternal Encounters*, p. 87.

36   Ogden, T. H. (2004). "An introduction to the reading of Bion." *The International Journal of Psychoanalysis*, 85(2), 285–300.

37   Ogden, "An introduction to the reading of Bion," p. 286.

38   Winnicott, D. W. (1991). *The Child, the Family, and the Outside World*. London, UK: Penguin.

39 Winnicott, D. W. (1949). "Hate in the counter-transference." *International Journal of Psychoanalysis*, *30*, 69.

40 Winnicott, "Hate in the counter-transference," pp. 73–74.

41 Winnicott, D. W. (1990). *The Maturational Processes and the Facilitating Environment: Studies in the Theory of Emotional Development*. London, UK: Karnac Books/Institute of Psycho-Analysis.

42 Winnicott, *The Maturational Processes and the Facilitating Environment*, p. 87.

43 Tronick, Ed, and Claudia M. Gold (2020). *The Power of Discord: Why the Ups and Downs of Relationships Are the Secret to Building Intimacy, Resilience, and Trust*. UK: Scribe.

44 Tronick and Gold, *The Power of Discord*, p. 37.

45 Lowy, Margo (2021). *The Maternal Experience: Encounters with Ambivalence and Love*. UK: Routledge.

46 Lowy, *The Maternal Experience*, p. 164.

47 Mihalich-Levin, Lori. "What Exactly IS Mom Guilt Anyway? A Clinical Psychotherapist Explains," Mindful Return, October 21, 2017, https://www.mindfulreturn.com/mom-guilt/.

48 Solomon, "Love: Paradox of Self and Other," p. 54.

49 Almond, *The Monster Within*, p. 4.

50 Edward, Joyce (2003). "A Mother's Hate: A Catalyst for Development," in Dale Mendell and Patsy Turrini (eds.), *The Inner World of the Mother*. Madison, CT: Psychosocial Press.

51 Edward, "A Mother's Hate," p. 248.

52 Rose, Jacqueline (2018). *Mothers: An Essay on Love and Cruelty*. New York, NY: Farrar, Straus and Giroux.

53 Rose, *Mothers: An Essay on Love and Cruelty*, p. 126.

54 Dubin, Minna. "The Rage Mothers Don't Talk About," *New York Times*, April 15, 2020, https://www.nytimes.com/2020/04/15/parenting/mother-rage.html.

55 Dubin, "The Rage Mothers Don't Talk About."

56 Mann, "In Search of Love and Hate," p. 45.

57 Mann, David (2002). "Introduction: The desire for love and hate (By way of a poetic polemic)," in David Mann (ed.), *Love and Hate: Psychoanalytic Perspectives*. East Sussex, UK: Brunner-Routledge.

58 Mann, "Introduction: The desire for love and hate," p. 8.

59 Winnicott, *The Maturational Processes and the Facilitating Environment*, p. 87.

60 *Little Fires Everywhere* (2020). Created by Liz Tigelaar [TV series]. Hulu.

61 de Marneffe, Daphne (2004). *Maternal Desire*. New York, NY: Back Bay Books.

62 de Marneffe, *Maternal Desire*, p. 124.

63 Sprenger, Stephanie and Jessica Smock (2015). *Mothering Through the Darkness: Women Open Up About the Postpartum Experience*. Berkeley, CA: She Writes Press.

64 Deutsch, J. "The Lessons I Learnt Facing Bell's Palsy with My First Born," The Grace Tales Team, March 26, 2021. Joh Deutsch interview, March 29, 2021.

65 "The Uncanny." *Little Fires Everywhere*, created by Liz Tigelaar, season 1, episode 5, Hulu. Original Streaming Date: April 8, 2020, https://press.hulu.com/shows/little-fires-everywhere/.

66 "Seventy Cents." *Little Fires Everywhere*, created by Liz Tigelaar, season 1, episode 3, Hulu. Original Streaming

Date: March 18, 2020, https://press.hulu.com/shows/little-fires-everywhere/.

67 Edward, "A Mother's Hate," p. 252.

68 Takševa, Tatjana (2017). "Mother Love, Maternal Ambivalence, and the Possibility of Empowered Mothering." *Hypatia: A Journal of Feminist Philosophy*, *32*(1).

69 Takševa, "Mother Love, Maternal Ambivalence, and the Possibility of Empowered Mothering," p. 161.

70 Takševa, "Mother Love, Maternal Ambivalence, and the Possibility of Empowered Mothering," p. 160.

71 Takševa, "Mother Love, Maternal Ambivalence, and the Possibility of Empowered Mothering," p. 162.

72 Takševa, "Mother Love, Maternal Ambivalence, and the Possibility of Empowered Mothering," p. 162.

73 Takševa, "Mother Love, Maternal Ambivalence, and the Possibility of Empowered Mothering," p. 162.

74 NICU: neonatal intensive care unit.

75 Takševa, "Mother Love, Maternal Ambivalence, and the Possibility of Empowered Mothering," p. 152.

76 Leach, Penelope (1980). *Your Baby & Child: From Birth to Age Five*. New York, NY: Alfred A. Knopf.

77 Almond, *The Monster Within*, p. 2.

78 Lowy, *The Maternal Experience*, p. 163.

79 Emma Heaphy (@words of_emmaheaphy), "It's no wonder we are made and broken simultaneously some days," Instagram, April 25, 2022, https://www.instagram.com/p/CcytRRFPc4x/.

80 Gibran, Kahlil (2022). *The Prophet*. Rye Brook, NY: Peter Pauper Press.

INDEX

ACKNOWLEDGMENTS

THANK YOU TO THE FOLLOWING people who've had a generous hand in bringing this book into the world:

Sarah Hochman, my editor, my guide, and my constant go-to person in all things writing. Sarah encourages me, makes me laugh, meets me where I am, and always knows where to find that missing doc, immediately.

Rebecca Sugar, who led me to Post Hill Press. Thanks to Anthony Ziccardi at Post Hill, who appreciated my topic and "got" this book from the get-go. To the staff at Post Hill, including especially Maddie Sturgeon, Holly Layman, and Alex Sturgeon who made such thoughtful and thorough edits to the final manuscript, and to Laura Yorke.

To my social media team, Molly Ebert, Megan McMullin, and special thanks to Shterny Dadon.

To all the mums who entrusted me with their stories and to Reese Witherspoon, who didn't call it by its name but gave a wonderful, spot-on performance of maternal ambivalence in *Little Fires Everywhere*.

To Jackie, for our daily and deep conversations about our six children, which buoy me.

To my husband David, who understands the reality and the value of all the bitter truths and loving moments.

ABOUT THE AUTHOR

DR. MARGO LOWY IS A psychotherapist with a specialty in mothering. In 2017, she completed her doctorate at the University of New South Wales in Sydney, Australia, investigating the field of maternal ambivalence. Dr. Lowy is the author of a previous academic book on the topic of maternal ambivalence, *The Maternal Experience: Encounters with Ambivalence and Love*, and has spoken on the subject at universities and media outlets in the United States, Australia, and Israel. She is a member of PEN America and a former advisor to the founder of the Australian Jewish Fertility Network (AJFN). She is mother to three children and is based with her husband in New York City. To learn more about her work, visit drmargolowy.com.